Introduction to Art
for
Toddlers and Preschoolers

Author: Katherine Karayiannis
Artwork & photography by Katherine Karayiannis

Published by The Preschool Art Expert LLC

© 2025 Katherine Karayiannis

Edition 1

Revised Publication date: 2026

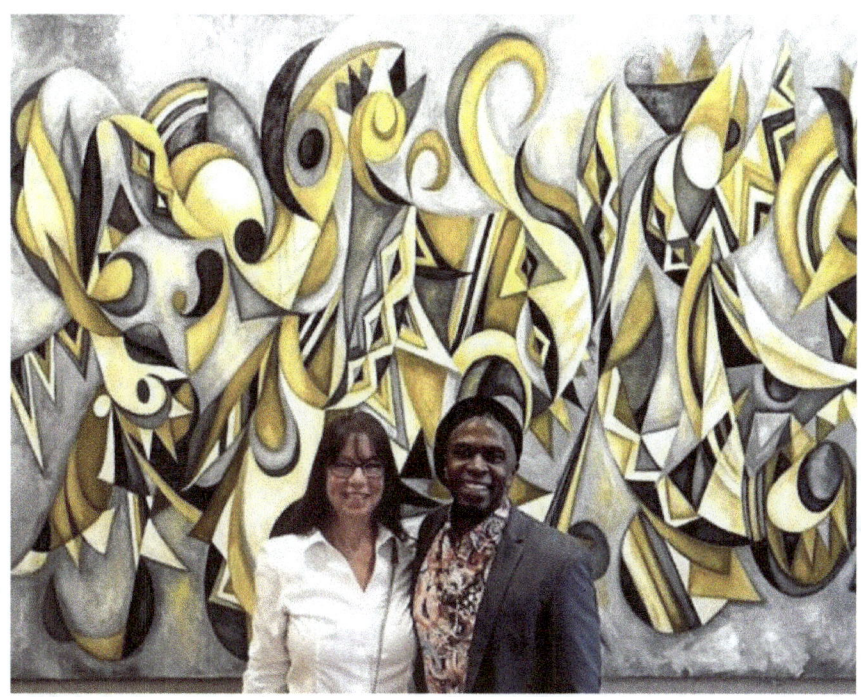

"As a visual artist and art educator specializing in painting, I constantly find new ways to connect with my students and art lovers. Katherine's three-part philosophy speaks to various levels of engagement for children of all ages. The Preschool Art Expert's identification of art in everyday life reinforces the specific lessons and vocabulary being learned and supports art appreciation. These are the connections that the arts can create that will last a lifetime. Art educators are cultural ambassadors who keep the arts alive, and Katherine does that with 'Introduction to Art for Toddlers & Preschoolers'. I highly recommend this book."

Cedric Michael Cox

Cedric Michael Cox is a well-respected, *nationally recognized artist*, best known for his unique style that merges surrealism and abstraction. Cedric has been creating and exhibiting his bright, colorful paintings for twenty-five years. He passes on his love for the arts by giving back to his community and working with students in many of the local school districts and several arts organizations. Cedric's large-scale murals can be seen in several neighborhoods in the Cincinnati area, where he has worked on beautification projects and with local businesses, including the Cincinnati Zoo. You can find Cedric's biography and work for sale at cedricmichaelcox.com

Introduction:

This book is an introduction to art. It was written for preschool teachers and parents. Anyone who wants an art education for their toddler or preschooler can use this book. You are the facilitator and partner in learning through experimentation and play.

Each successive book gives your child more responsibility as his or her art skills increase. As you explore each activity, you will be partners in experimentation and discovery. As you interact, you will use your imaginations to implement suggestions for each activity, while coming up with your own unique additions that fit your learning goals and abilities.

This book is meant to be used to teach and learn art and each child will progress at his or her own pace. Activities can be followed in the given sequence or mixed or skipped. Your children and students will develop skills while having fun! Give credit for every effort, as each piece is beautiful! *Remember – It doesn't have to be perfect!*

This book is comprehensive and developmentally, age appropriate. Each unit focuses on basic skills, teaches vocabulary words, addresses different learning styles, shows connections between art and other subjects and has an accompanying activity, book or artist. Learning is meant to occur through exploration, experimentation and play as you manipulate materials.

Each accompanying activity makes a **REAL-WORLD CONNECTION TO SHOW CHILDREN HOW ART RELATES TO THEIR DAILY LIVES AND REINFORCE LEARNING**!

Features:

Each Unit will include the following:

- Unit Introduction and description.

- List of vocabulary words corresponding to the activities in the unit. Practice these words with your child.

- Learning styles and senses children will use during the lesson.

- Learning connections to other subjects.

- An accompanying activity that will *reinforce learning* and *make a real-world connection*, found at the bottom of each page.

HAVE FUN!

Table of Contents

Unit One: Shapes and Primary colors
Introduction and explanation

The focus is on basic skills, covering the geometric shapes circle, square, triangle *and* the Primary colors red, blue, and yellow. We sing throughout the unit to help children remember information with rhythm. Children love to sing and create! You will find them asking to do these activities over and over!

Encourage your child to repeat the vocabulary words as you talk about each activity.

Vocabulary

Red   Circle ◯

Blue   Square ▢

Yellow   Triangle △

Learning styles addressed

Visual
Auditory
Kinesthetic

Learning connections

Art - colors: red, blue, yellow

Geometry - shapes: circle, square, triangle

Language arts / *phonics*: sound R, sound B, sound Y, rhyme

Music - singing and rhythm

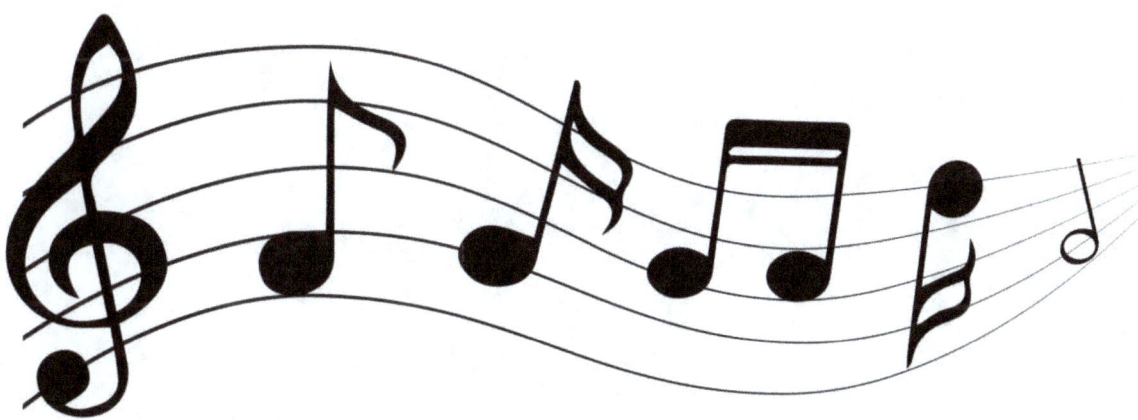

Unit 1: Shapes and Primary colors

Activity #1 – Hand paint a red circle

FOCUS:
Color: red
Shape: circle
Letter: R

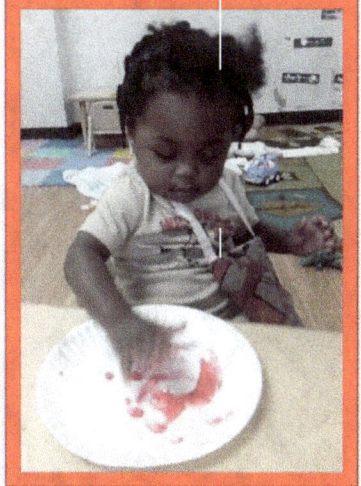

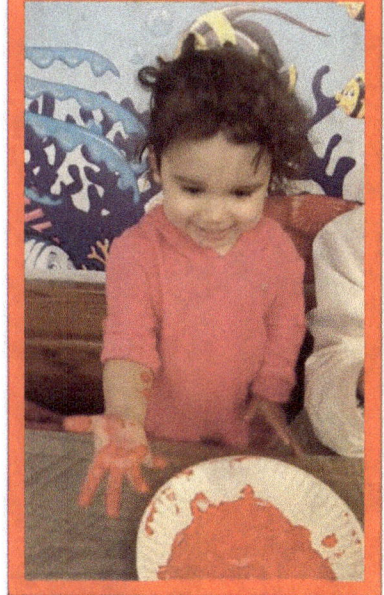

MATERIALS:
paper
plate
red
paint
wipes
surface protector

Instructions:

1. Put down the surface protector.
2. Lay out the paper plate.
3. Pour some red paint on the paper plate.
4. Dip your child's hands into the red paint.
5. While singing to the tune of "wheels on the Bus", sing these lyrics:
   "My little red hands go round and round, round and round, round and round. My little red hands go round and round. Look now I've made a circle."
6. While singing, encourage child to make hands go around the inside of the plate and fill in the whole circle with red.
7. Encourage your child to sing along!
8. When you are finished painting, use the wipes to get the paint off your child's hands.

Making real-world connections with an
Accompanying activity, to reinforce learning and show children how art relates to their daily lives.

- *Activity:* Identify colors and shapes in the environment.
- *YouTube Video:* The Kandinsky Effect.

Unit 1: Shapes and Primary colors

Activity #2 – Hand paint a blue circle

FOCUS:
Color: blue
Shape: circle
Letter: B

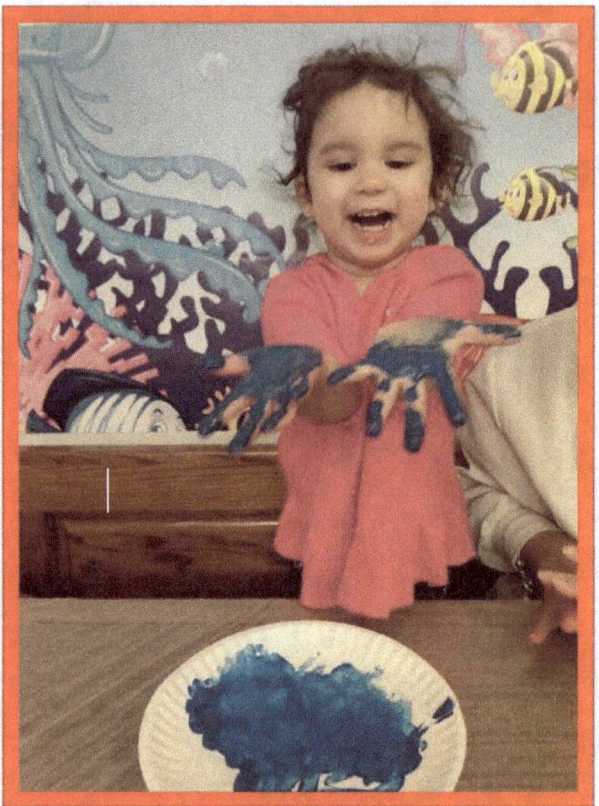

MATERIALS:
paper
plate
blue
paint
wipes
surface protector

Instructions:

1. Put down the surface protector.
2. Lay out the paper plate.
3. Pour some blue paint on the paper plate.
4. Dip your child's hands into the blue paint.
5. While singing to the tune of "wheels on the Bus", sing these lyrics:
   "My bouncy blue hands go round and round, round and round, round and round. My bouncy blue hands go round and round. Look now I've made a circle."
6. While singing, encourage your child to make hands go around the inside of the plate and fill in the whole circle with blue.
7. Encourage your child to sing along!
8. When you are finished painting, use the wipes to get the paint off your child's hands.

Making real-world connections with an
Accompanying activity, **to reinforce learning and show children how art relates to their daily lives.**

- *Activity:* **Identify colors and shapes in the environment.**
- *YouTube Video:* **The Kandinsky Effect.**

Unit 1: Shapes and Primary colors

Activity #3 – Hand paint a yellow circle

FOCUS:
Color: yellow
Shape: circle
Letter: Y

MATERIALS:
paper plate
yellow paint
wipes
surface protector

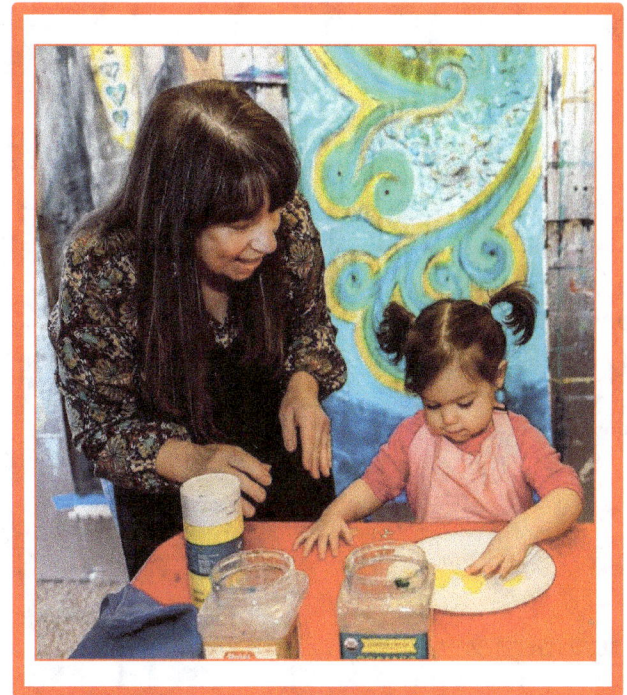

Instructions:

1. Put down the surface protector.
2. Lay out the paper plate.
3. Pour some yellow paint onto the paper plate.
4. Dip your child's hands into the yellow paint.
5. While singing to the tune of "wheels on the Bus", sing these lyrics:
   "My young yellow hands go round and round, round, and round, round, and round. My young yellow hands go round and round. Look now I've made a circle."
6. While singing, encourage child to make hands go around the inside the shape of the paper plate and fill in the whole circle with yellow.
7. Encourage your child to sing along!
8. When you are finished painting, use the wipes to get the paint off your child's hands.

Making real-world connections with an
Accompanying activity, to reinforce learning and show children how art relates to their daily lives.

- *Activity:* Identify colors and shapes in the environment.
- *YouTube Video:* The Kandinsky Effect.

Unit 1 : Shapes and Primary colors

Activity #4 – Hand paint a red square

FOCUS:
Color:red
Shape: square

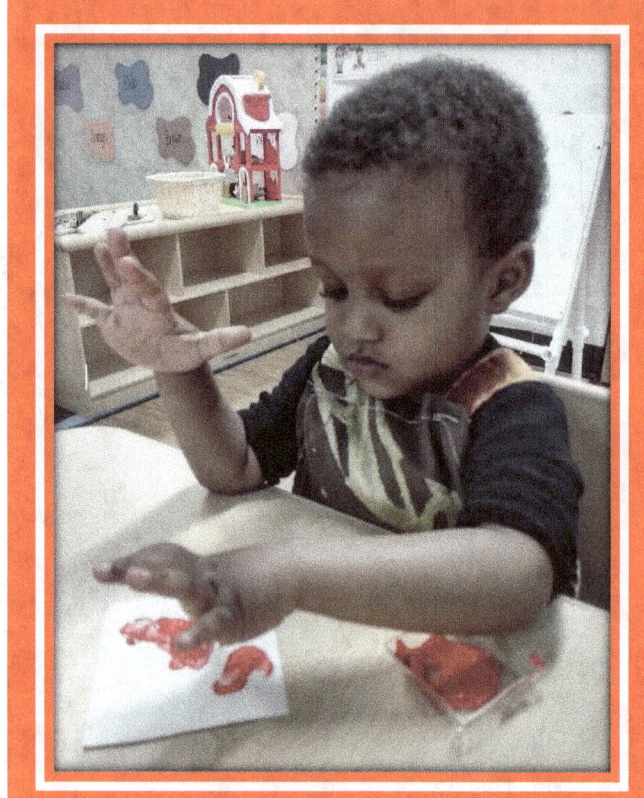

MATERIALS:
paper or cardboard square
red paint
wipes
surface protector

Instructions:

1. Lay out the surface protector.
2. Lay out the paper square.
3. Pour some red paint onto the square.
4. Recite this simple rhyme:
   "Square, square, I see you there. Four sides, four corners make a square."
5. While reciting the rhyme, encourage child to make hands go around the square to fill it in with red.
6. Encourage your child to sing along!
7. When you are finished painting, use the wipes to get the paint off your child's hands.

Making real-world connections with an
Accompanying activity, to reinforce learning and show children how art relates to their daily lives.

- *Activity:* **Identify colors and shapes in the environment.**
- *YouTube Video:* **Mondrian Animation.**
  Mondrian Animation is a video that is representative of Mondrian's style. It shows many squares and rectangles, so as you and your child watch it, you can easily identify the shapes.

Unit 1: Shapes and Primary colors

Activity #5 – Hand paint a blue square

FOCUS:
Color: blue
Shape: square

MATERIALS:
paper or cardboard square
blue paint
wipes
surface protector

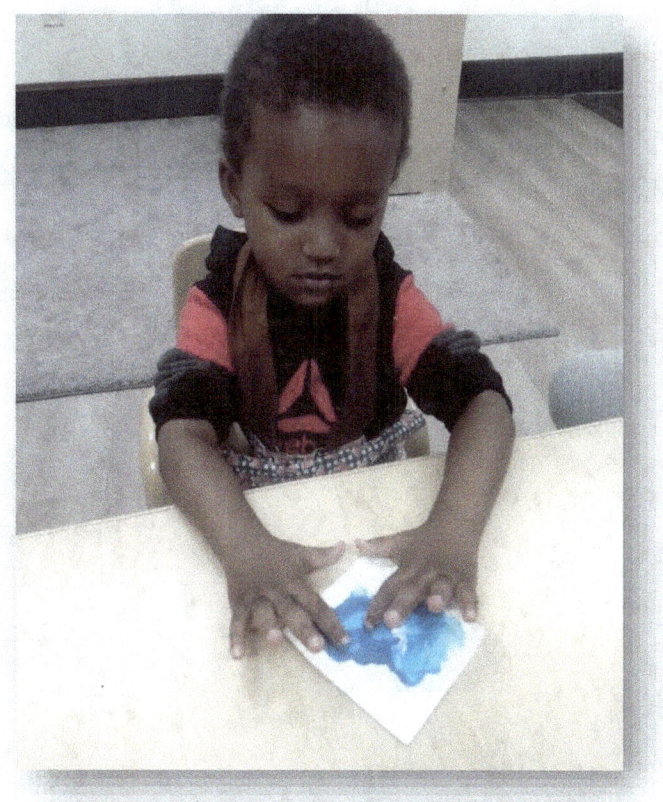

Instructions:

1. Lay out the surface protector.
2. Lay out the paper square.
3. Pour some blue paint onto the square.
4. Recite this simple rhyme:
   "Square, square, I see you there. Four sides, four corners make a square."
5. While reciting the rhyme, encourage child to make hands go around the square to fill it in with blue.
6. Encourage your child to sing along!
7. When you are finished painting, use the wipes to get the paint off your child's hands.

Making real-world connections with an
Accompanying activity, to reinforce learning and show children how art relates to their daily lives.

- *Activity:* **Identify colors and shapes in the environment.**
- *YouTube Video:* **Mondrian Animation**

Mondrian Animation is a video that is representative of Mondrian's style. It shows many squares and rectangles so, as you and your child watch it, you can easily identify the shape

Unit 1: Shapes and Primary colors

Activity #6 – Hand paint a yellow square

FOCUS:
Color: yellow
Shape: square

MATERIALS:
paper or cardboard square
yellow paint
wipes
surface protector

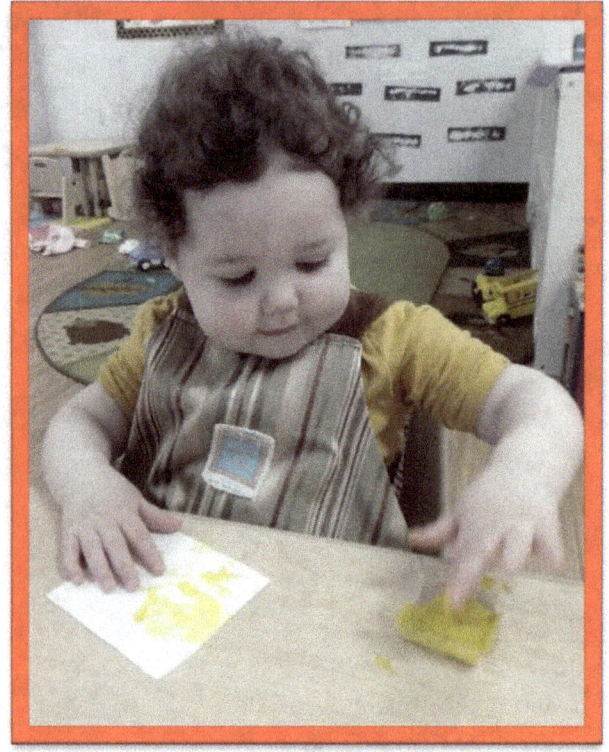

Instructions:

1. Lay out the surface protector.
2. Lay out the paper square.
3. Pour some yellow paint onto the square.
4. Recite this simple rhyme:
   "Square, square, I see you there. Four sides, four corners make a square."
5. While reciting the rhyme, encourage child to make hands go around the square to fill it in with yellow.
6. When you are finished painting, use the wipes to get the paint off your child's hands.

Making real-world connections with an

Accompanying activity, to reinforce learning and show children how art relates to their daily lives.

- *Activity:* Identify colors and shapes in the environment.
- *YouTube Video:* Mondrian Animation
  Mondrian Animation is a video that is representative of Mondrian's style. It shows many squares and rectangles so, as you and your child watch it, you can easily identify the shapes.

Unit 1: Shapes and Primary colors

Activity #7 – Hand paint a red triangle

FOCUS:
Color: red
Shape: triangle

MATERIALS:
paper or cardboard triangle
red paint
wipes

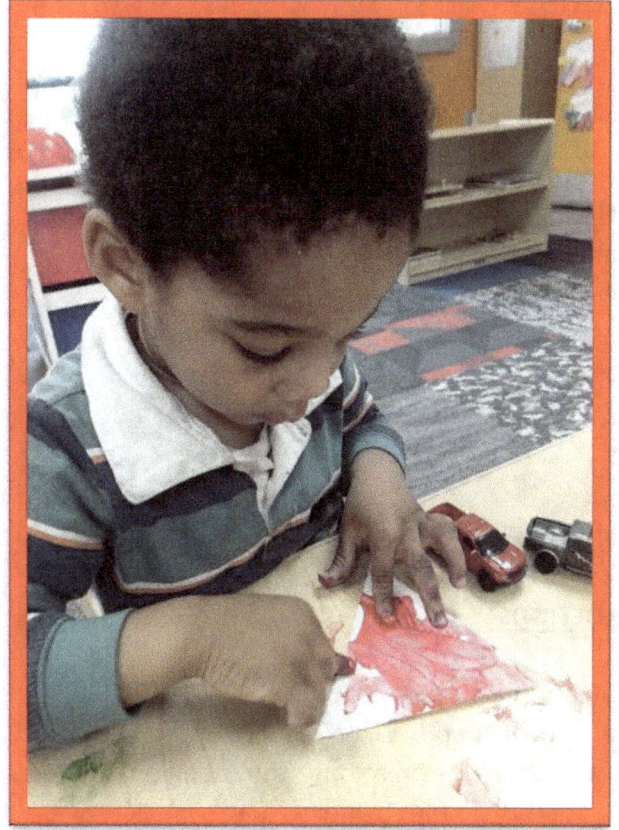

Instructions:

1. Lay out the surface protector.
2. Lay out the paper or cardboard triangle.
3. Pour some red paint onto the triangle.
4. Recite this simple rhyme:
   "I see a triangle happy as can be. Corners you have them, 1,2,3."
5. While reciting the rhyme, encourage child to make hands go around the triangle to fill it in with red.
6. When you are finished painting, use the wipes to get the paint off your child's hands.

Making real-world connections with an
Accompanying activity, to reinforce learning and show children how art relates to their daily lives.

- *Activity*: Identify colors and shapes in the environment.
- *Reading:* The tiny Traveler, Egypt: A book of shapes

Unit 1: Shapes and Primary colors

Activity #8 – Hand paint a blue triangle

FOCUS:
Color: blue
Shape: triangle

MATERIALS:
surface protector
paper or cardboard triangle
blue paint
wipes

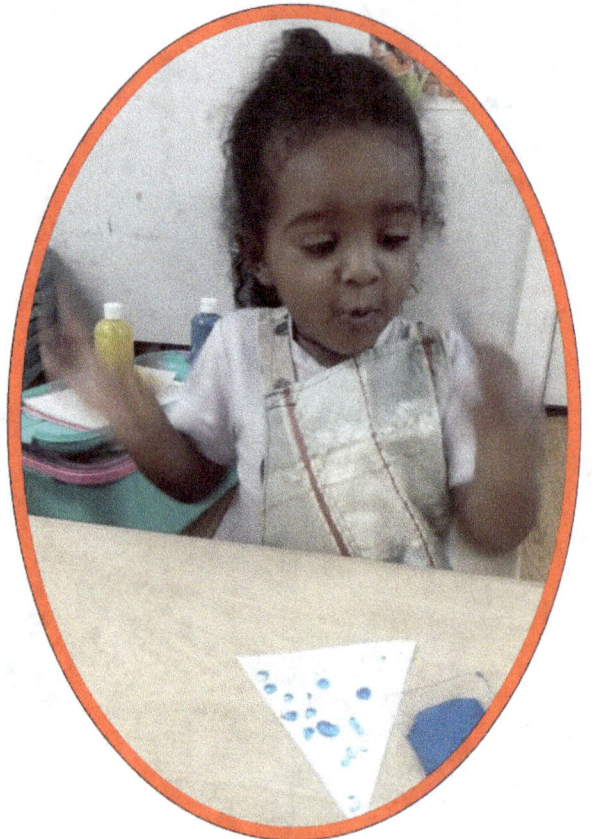

Instructions:

1. Lay out the surface protector.
2. Lay out the paper triangle.
3. Pour some blue paint onto the triangle.
4. Recite this simple rhyme:
   "I see a triangle happy as can be. Corners you have them, 1,2,3."
5. While reciting the rhyme, encourage child to make hands go around the triangle to fill it in with blue.
6. When you are finished painting, use the wipes to get the paint off your child's hands.

Making real-world connections with an
Accompanying activity, to reinforce learning and show children how art relates to their daily lives.

- *Activity:* Identify colors and shapes in the environment
- *Reading:* The tiny Traveler, Egypt: A book of shapes

Unit 1: Shapes and Primary colors

Activity #9 – Hand paint a yellow triangle

FOCUS:
Color: yellow
Shape: triangle

MATERIALS:
surface protector
paper or cardboard triangle
yellow paint
wipes

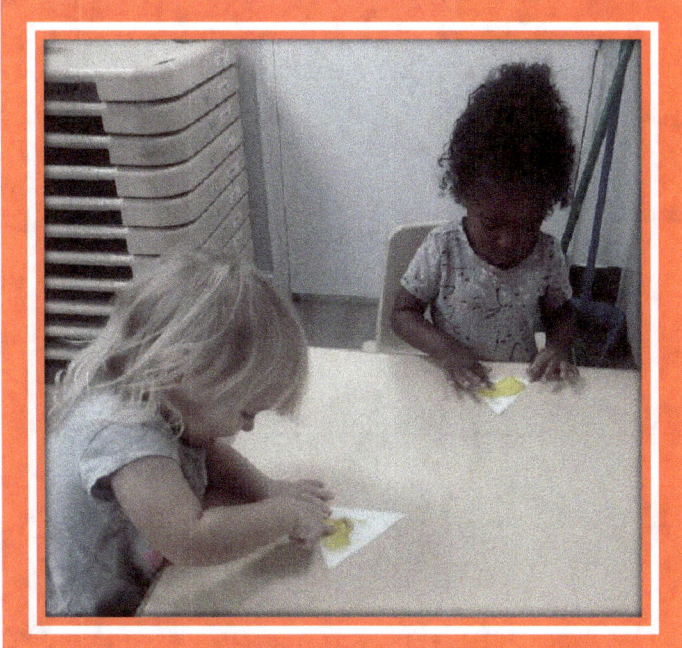

Instructions:

1. Lay out the surface protector.
2. Lay out the paper triangle.
3. Pour some yellow paint onto the triangle.
4. Recite this simple rhyme:
    "I see a triangle happy as can be. Corners you have them, 1,2,3."
5. While reciting the rhyme, encourage child to make hands go around the triangle to fill it in with yellow.
6. When you are finished painting, use the wipes to get the paint off your child's hand.

Making real-world connections with an
Accompanying activity, to reinforce learning and show children how art relates to their daily lives.

- *Activity:* **Identify colors and shapes in the environment**
- *Reading:* **The tiny Traveler, Egypt: A book of shapes**

Unit Two: Shapes and secondary colors
Introduction and explanation

The focus is on basic skills, covering the shapes oval, rectangle and star *and* the Secondary colors green, orange, and purple. We sing throughout the unit to help children remember information with rhythm. Children love to sing and create! You will find them asking to do these activities over and over!

Encourage your child to repeat the vocabulary words as you talk about each activity.

Vocabulary

Green   Oval
Orange   Rectangle
Purple   Star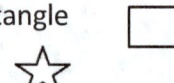

Learning styles addressed

Visual

 Auditory

Kinesthetic

Learning connections

Art - colors: green, orange, purple

Geometry - shapes: oval, rectangle, star

Music - singing and rhythm

Unit Two: Shapes and secondary colors

Activity #1 – Hand paint a green oval

FOCUS:
Color: green
Shape: oval

MATERIALS:
surface protector
paper or cardboard oval
green paint
wipes

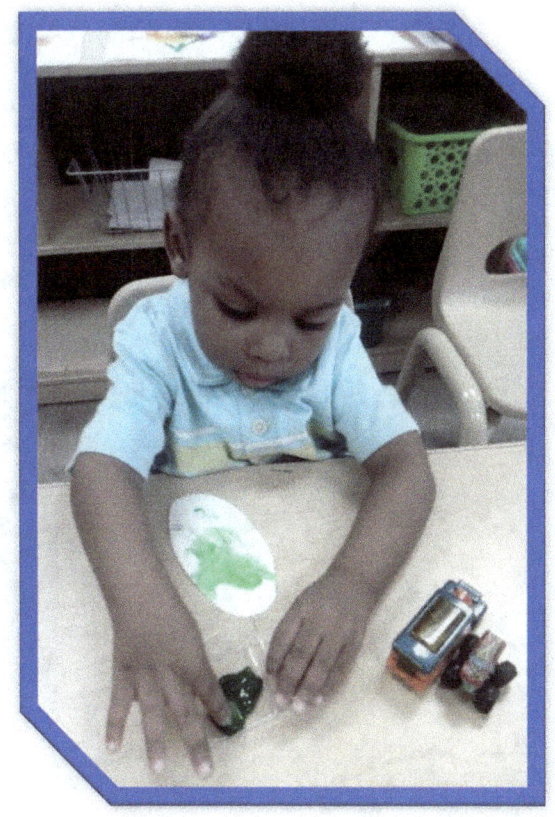

Instructions:

1. Lay out the surface protector.
2. Lay out the paper or cardboard oval.
3. Pour some green paint on the oval.
4. Let your child use hands and fingers to paint the oval green.
5. Say "this is an oval. It looks like an egg."
6. Saying the name of the shape as you are painting will reinforce your child's learning.
7. When you are finished painting, use the wipes to get the paint off your child's hands.

Making real-world connections with an
Accompanying activity, to reinforce learning and show children how art relates to their daily lives.

- *Activity:* **Identify colors and shapes in the environment**.
- *Activity:* **What can you find that is an oval shape? Eggs.**

Unit Two: Shapes and secondary colors

Activity #2– Hand paint an orange oval

FOCUS:
Color: orange
Shape: oval

MATERIALS:
surface protector
paper or cardboard oval
orange paint
wipes

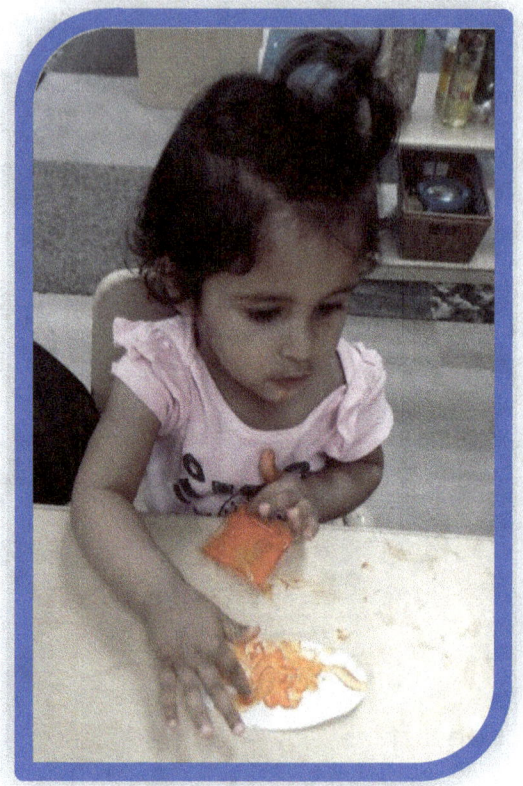

Instructions:

1. Lay out the surface protector.
2. Lay out the paper or cardboard oval.
3. Pour some orange paint on the oval.
4. Let your child use hands and fingers to paint oval orange.
   Say, "This is an oval. It looks like an egg."
5. Saying the name of the shape as you are painting will reinforce your child's learning.
6. When you are finished painting, use the wipes to get the paint off your child's hands.

Making real-world connections with an
Accompanying activity, to reinforce learning and show children how art relates to their daily lives.

- *Activity:* Identify colors and shapes in the environment.
- *Activity:* What can you find that is an oval shape? Eggs.

Unit Two: Shapes and secondary colors

Activity #3 – Hand paint a purple oval

FOCUS:
Color: purple
Shape: oval

MATERIALS:
surface protector
paper or cardboard oval
purple paint
wipes

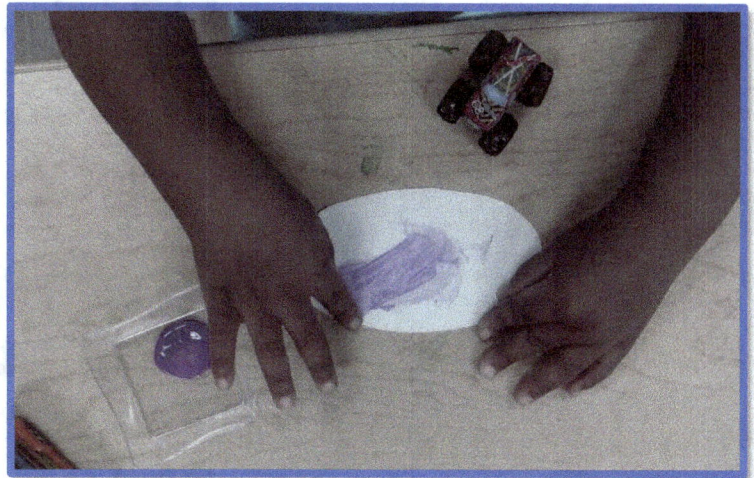

Instructions:

1. Lay out the surface protector.
2. Lay out the paper or cardboard oval.
3. Pour some purple paint on the oval.
4. Let your child use hands and fingers to paint the oval purple.
5. Say, "This is an oval. It looks like an egg."
6. Saying the name of the shape as you are painting will reinforce your child's learning.
7. When you are finished painting, use the wipes to get the paint off your child's hands.

Making real-world connections with an
Accompanying activity, to reinforce learning and show children how art relates to their daily lives.

- *Activity:* **Identify colors and shapes in the environment.**
- *Activity:* **What can you find that is an oval shape? Eggs.**

Unit Two: Shapes and secondary colors

Activity #4 – Hand paint a green rectangle

FOCUS:
Color: green
Shape: rectangle

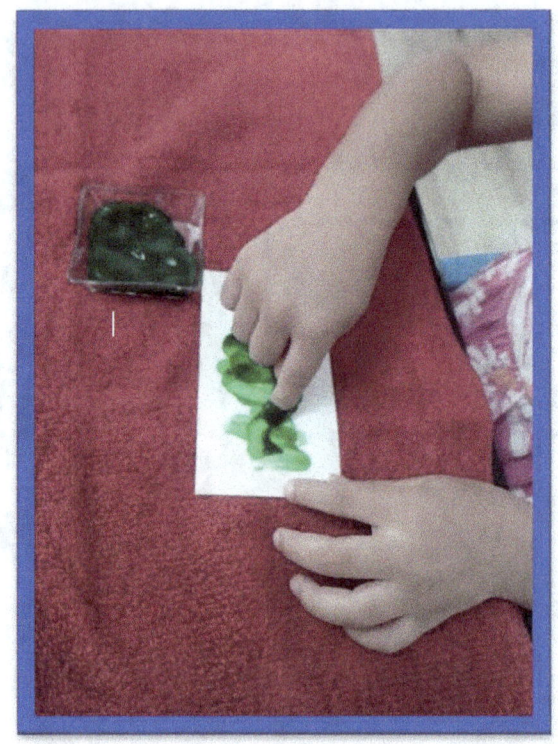

MATERIALS:
surface protector
paper or cardboard
rectangle green paint
wipes

Instructions:

1. Lay out the surface protector.
2. Lay out the paper or cardboard rectangle.
3. Pour some green paint on the rectangle.
4. Let your child use hands and fingers to paint the rectangle green.
5. As you are painting, you can say, "Rectangle, rectangle, I see a rectangle".
6. Saying the name of the shape as you are painting will reinforce your child's learning.
7. When you are finished painting, use the wipes to get the paint off your child's hands.

Making real-world connections with an
Accompanying activity, to reinforce learning and show children how art relates to their daily lives.

- *Activity:* **Identify colors and shapes in the environment.**
- *Activity:* **What can you find that is a rectangle shape? The door.**

Unit Two: Shapes and secondary colors

Activity #5 – Hand paint an orange rectangle

> **FOCUS:**
> Color: orange
> Shape: rectangle

> **MATERIALS:**
> surface protector
> paper or cardboard rectangle
> orange paint
> wipes

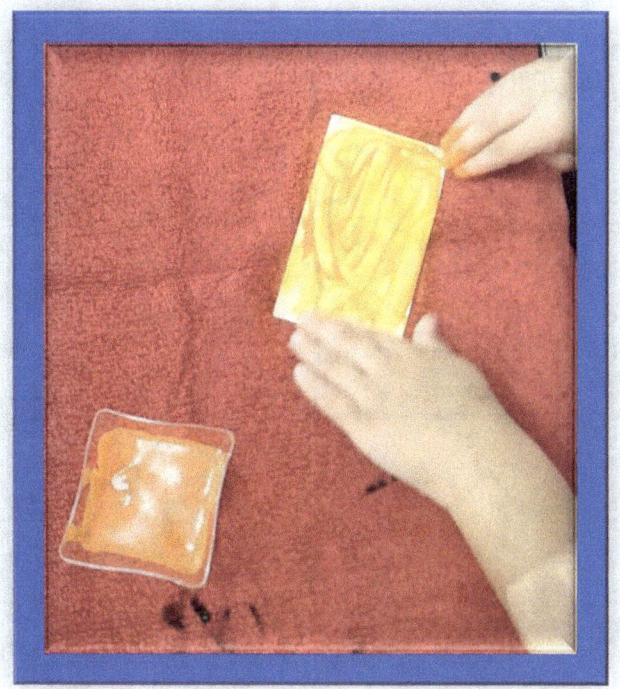

Instructions:

1. Lay out the surface protector.
2. Lay out the paper or cardboard rectangle.
3. Pour some orange paint on the rectangle.
4. Let your child use hands and fingers to paint the rectangle orange.
5. As you are painting, you can say, "Rectangle, rectangle, I see a rectangle".
6. Saying the name of the shape as you are painting will reinforce your child's learning.
7. When you are finished painting, use the wipes to get the paint off your child's hands.

Making real-world connections with an
Accompanying activity, to reinforce learning and show children how art relates to their daily lives.

- *Activity:* **Identify colors and shapes in the environment.**
- *Activity:* **What can you find that is a rectangle shape? The door.**

Unit 2: Shapes and secondary colors

Activity # 6 Hand paint a purple rectangle

FOCUS:
Color: purple
Shape: rectangle

MATERIALS:
surface protector
paper or cardboard rectangle
purple paint
wipes

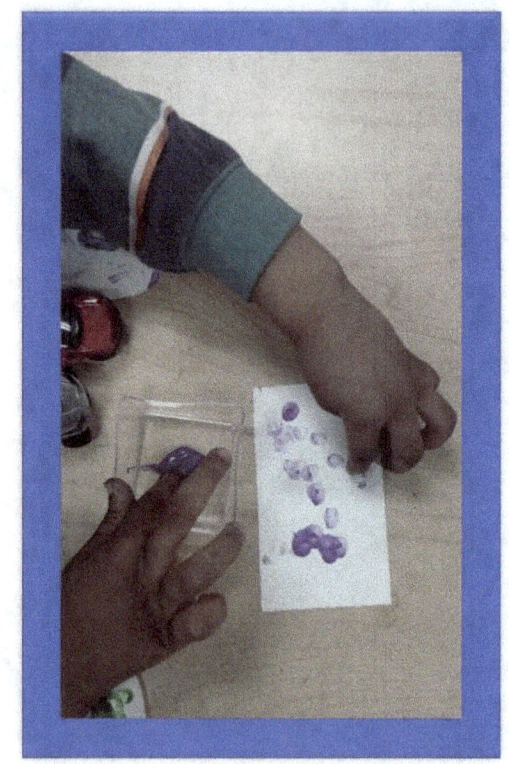

Instructions:

1. Lay out the surface protector.
2. Lay out the paper rectangle.
3. Pour some purple paint on the rectangle.
4. Let your child use hands and fingers to paint the rectangle purple.
5. As you are painting, you can say, "Rectangle, rectangle, I see a rectangle".
6. Saying the name of the shape as you are painting will reinforce your child's learning.
7. When you are finished painting, use the wipes to get the paint off your child's hands.

Making real-world connections with an
Accompanying activity, to reinforce learning and show children how art relates to their daily lives.

- *Activity:* **Identify colors and shapes in the environment.**
- *Activity:* **What can you find that is a rectangle shape? The door.**

Unit 2: Shapes and secondary colors

Activity # 7 Hand paint a green star

FOCUS:
Color: green
Shape: star

MATERIALS:
surface protector
paper or cardboard star
green paint
wipes

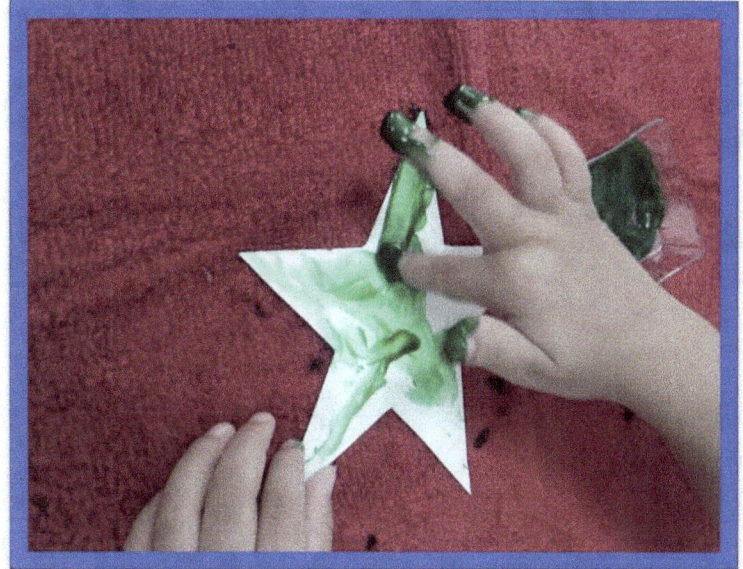

Instructions:

1. Lay out the surface protector.
2. Lay out the paper or cardboard star.
3. Pour some green paint on the star.
4. Let your child use hands and fingers to paint the star green.
6. Recite this simple rhyme:
    "Star, star, I see you from afar. I look up and there you are."
7. Saying the name of the shape as you are painting will reinforce your child's learning.
8. When you are finished painting, use the wipes to get the paint off your child's hands.

Making real-world connections with an
Accompanying activity, to reinforce learning and show children how art relates to
their daily lives.

- *Activity:* **Identify colors and shapes in the environment.**
- *Activity:* **Look up at the night sky and see if you can find any stars.**

Unit 2: Shapes and secondary colors

Activity #8 – Hand painting an orange star

FOCUS:
Color: orange
Shape: star

MATERIALS:
surface protector
paper or cardboard star
orange paint
wipes

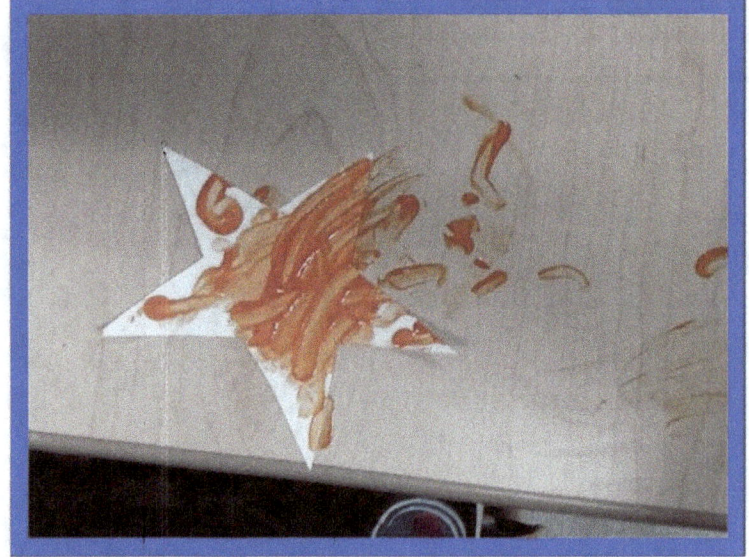

Instructions:

1. Lay out the surface protector.
2. Lay out the paper or cardboard star.
3. Pour some orange paint on the star.
4. Let your child use hands and fingers to paint the star orange.
5. Recite this simple rhyme:
    "Star, star, I see you from afar. I look up and there you are."
6. Saying the name of the shape as you are painting will reinforce your child's learning.
7. When you are finished painting, use the wipes to get the paint off your child's hands.

Making real-world connections with an
Accompanying activity, to reinforce learning and show children how art relates to their daily lives.

- *Activity:* **Identify colors and shapes in the environment.**
- *Activity:* **Look up at the night sky and see if you can find any stars.**

Unit 2: Shapes and secondary colors

Activity #9 – Hand painting a purple star

FOCUS:
Color: purple
Shape: star

MATERIALS:
surface protector
paper or cardboard star
purple paint
wipes

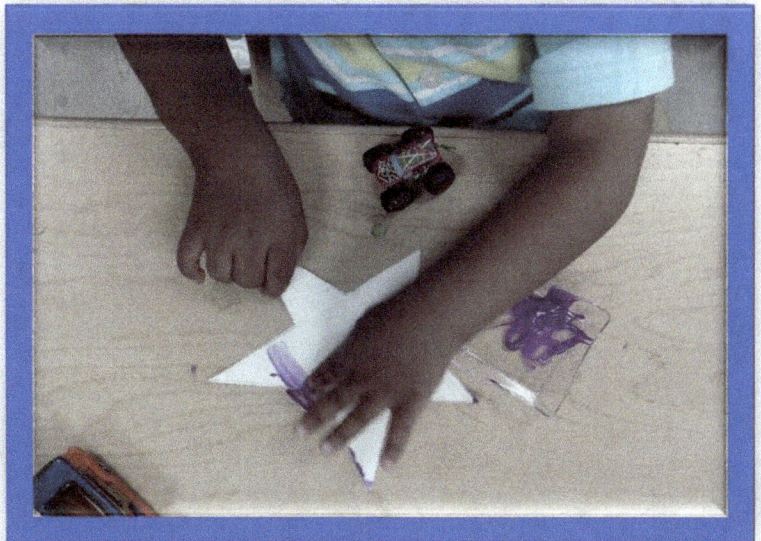

Instructions:

1. Lay out the surface protector.
2. Lay out the paper or cardboard star.
3. Pour some purple paint on the star.
4. Let your child use hands and fingers to paint the star purple.
5. Recite this simple rhyme:
   "Star, star, I see you from afar. I look up and there you are.
6. Saying the name of the shape as you are painting will reinforce your child's learning.
7. When you are finished painting, use the wipes to get the paint off your child's hands

---

Making real-world connections with an
Accompanying activity, to reinforce learning and show children how art relates to their daily lives.

- *Activity:* **Identify colors and shapes in the environment.**
- *Activity:* **Look up at the night sky and see if you can find any stars.**

Unit Three: Shapes and Primary colors
Introduction and explanation

The focus is on basic skills, covering the Secondary colors green, orange, and purple. We mix colors to create creatures in the environment and learn to identify the creatures of Spring. Children will have fun and get messy as they practice identifying each color.

Encourage your child to repeat the vocabulary words as you talk about each activity.

Vocabulary

Green	butterfly	grasshopper
Orange	beetle	glacier
Purple		

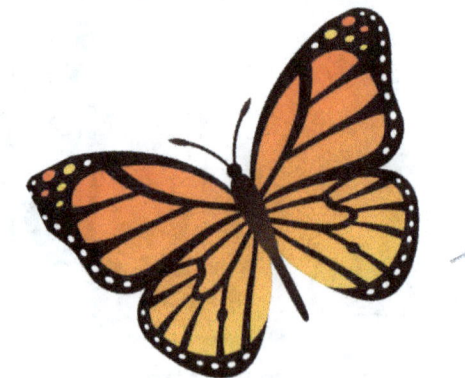

Learning styles addressed

Visual
Kinesthetic

Learning connections

Art - colors: green, orange, purple
  texture: feel of the shaving
  cream (Or whipped cream)

Science – plants: grass, flowers
  environment: sun, glacier
  insects: butterfly, beetle, grasshopper

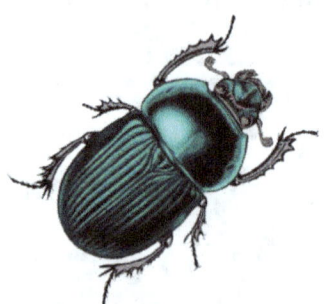

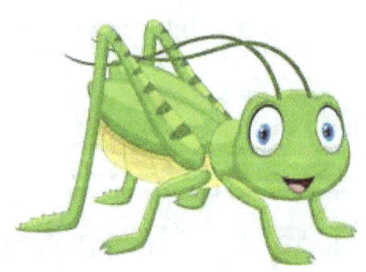

Unit #3: Mixing Secondary colors

Activity #1 – Mixing Primary colors to make green

FOCUS:
Mixing the Primary colors yellow and blue to make green

MATERIALS: yellow paint
surface protector   blue paint
shaving cream   wipes

Whipped cream & food coloring can be substituted for the shaving cream and paint!

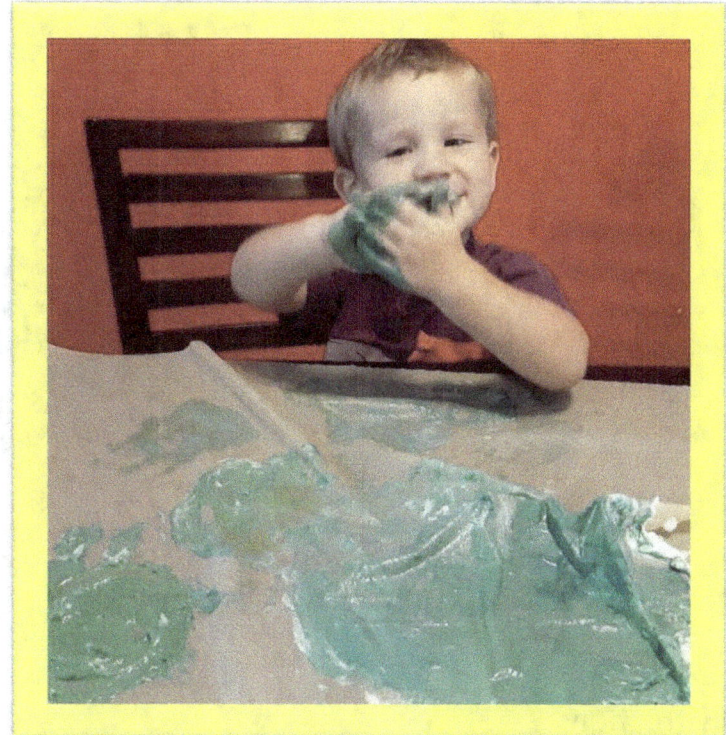

Instructions:

1. Lay out the surface protector.
2. Spray two piles of shaving cream on the table.
3. Add drops of yellow to one pile.
4. Add drops of blue to the other pile.
5. Have your child mix and blend the two piles of shaving cream together until it turns green.

Making real-world connections with an
Accompanying activity, to reinforce learning and show children how art relates to their daily lives.

- *Activity:* **Walk outside and identify things that are green.**

Unit #3: Mixing Secondary colors

Activity #2 – Mixing Primary colors to make orange

FOCUS:
Mixing the Primary colors red and yellow to make orange

MATERIALS:
surface protector
shaving cream
red paint
yellow paint

Whipped cream & food coloring can be substituted for the shaving cream and paint!

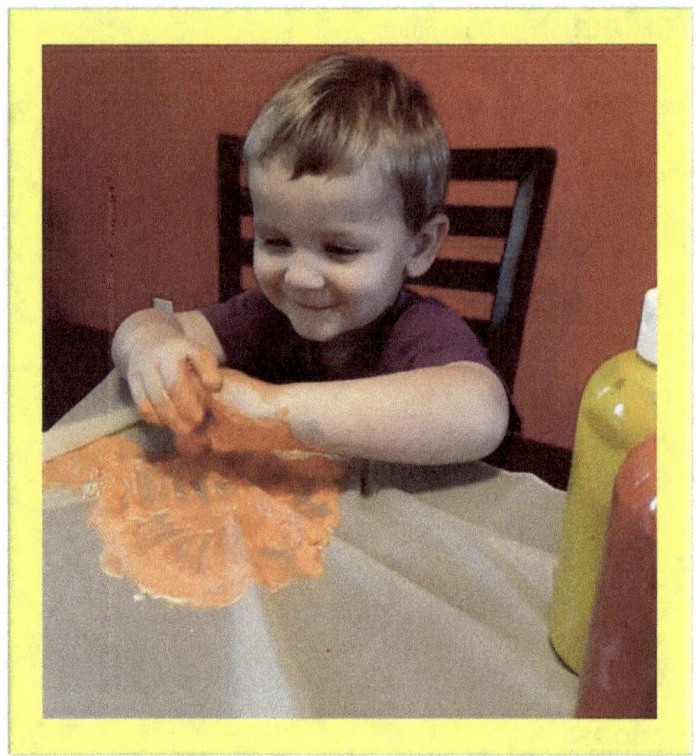

Instructions:

1. Lay out the surface protector.
2. Spray two piles of shaving cream on the table.
3. Add drops of yellow to one pile.
4. Add drops of red to the other pile.
5. Have your child mix and blend the two piles of shaving cream together until it turns orange.

Making real-world connections with an
Accompanying activity, to reinforce learning and show children how art relates to their daily lives.

- *Activity:* **Walk outside and identify things that are orange.**

Unit #3: Mixing Secondary colors

Activity #3 – Mixing Primary colors to make purple

FOCUS:
Mixing the Primary colors red and blue to make purple

MATERIALS:
surface protector
shaving cream
red paint
blue paint

Whipped cream & food coloring can be substituted for the shaving cream and paint!

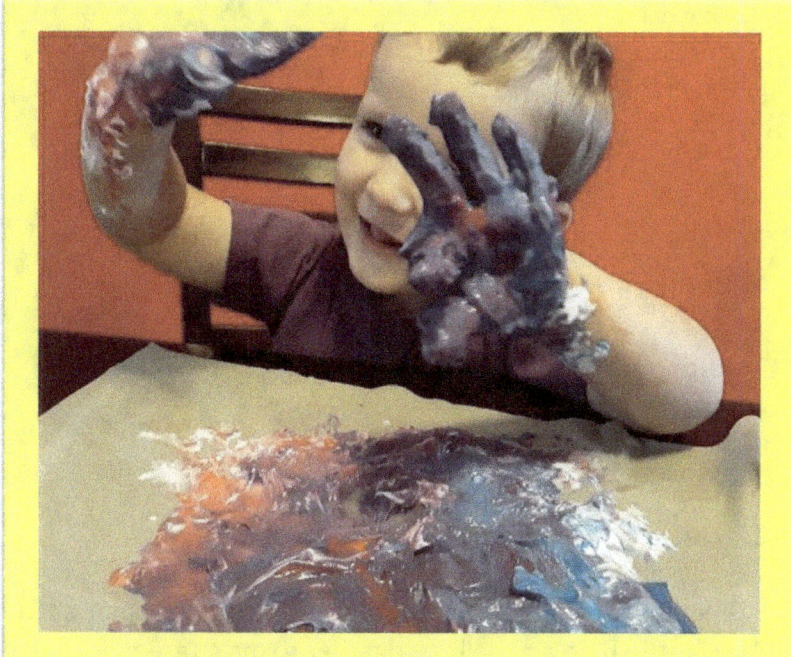

Instructions:

1. Lay out the surface protector.
2. Spray two piles of shaving cream on the table.
3. Add drops of red to one pile.
4. Add drops of blue to the other pile.
5. Have your child mix and blend the two piles until it turns purple.

Making real-world connections with an *Accompanying activity,* to reinforce learning and show children how art relates to their daily lives.

- *Activity:* **Walk outside and identify things that are purple.**

Unit #3: Mixing Secondary colors

Activity #4 – Painting a Spring Scene with Secondary colors

FOCUS: mixing Primary colors to make Secondary colors

MATERIALS:
surface protector
red paint
blue paint
yellow paint
paper plate
sheet of paper
q-tips

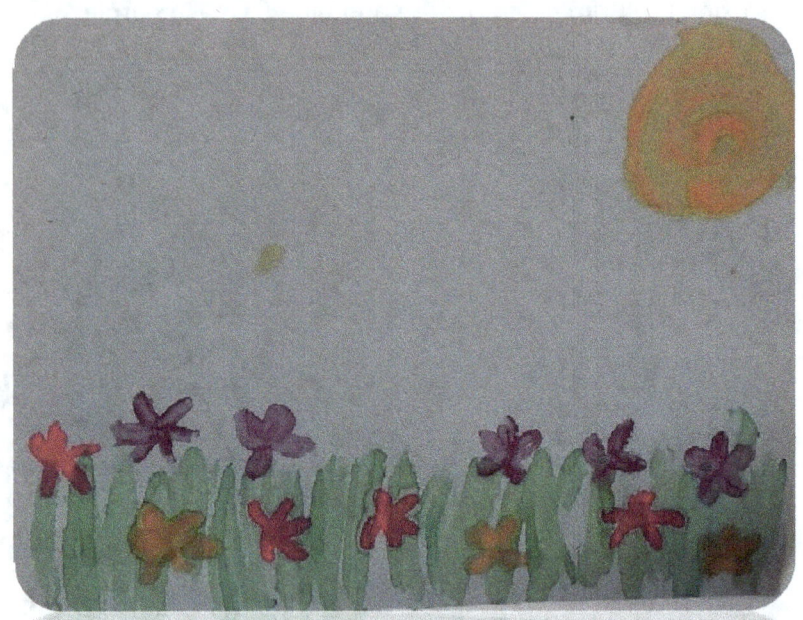

Instructions:

1. Lay out the surface protector.
2. Set out the paper plate and sheet of paper.
3. Pour a small cookie sized shape of each color paint onto the paper plate.
4. Mix the blue and yellow together to make green for the grass.
5. Paint the grass on the bottom of the paper with fingers.
6. Mix the red and yellow to make orange for the sun.
7. Paint the sun on the top of the paper with fingers.
8. Mix some red and blue to make purple for flowers.
9. Use Q-tips to paint red, orange and purple flowers in the grass.
10. Your child will have such a feeling of accomplishment – like they've created a true masterpiece!

Making real-world connections with an
Accompanying activity, to reinforce learning and show children how art relates to their daily lives.

- *Activity:* Go for a walk and look at your surroundings. Ask your child to describe your surroundings to you.

Unit #3: Mixing Secondary colors

Activity #5 – Making a Monarch Butterfly

FOCUS: mixing Primary colors red and yellow to make orange

MATERIALS:
surface protector
paper plate
red paint
yellow paint
black paint
Q-tips
Googly eyes
Pipe cleaner or ribbon for
antenae

Since my first publication of this book, the Monarch population is reaching extinction. We can all help by planting a Milkweed bush in our yards/ gardens. This is the only plant the Monarch will lay eggs on and the only food for it's caterpillars. How amazing it would be to attract a Monarch to your yard for your child to see!

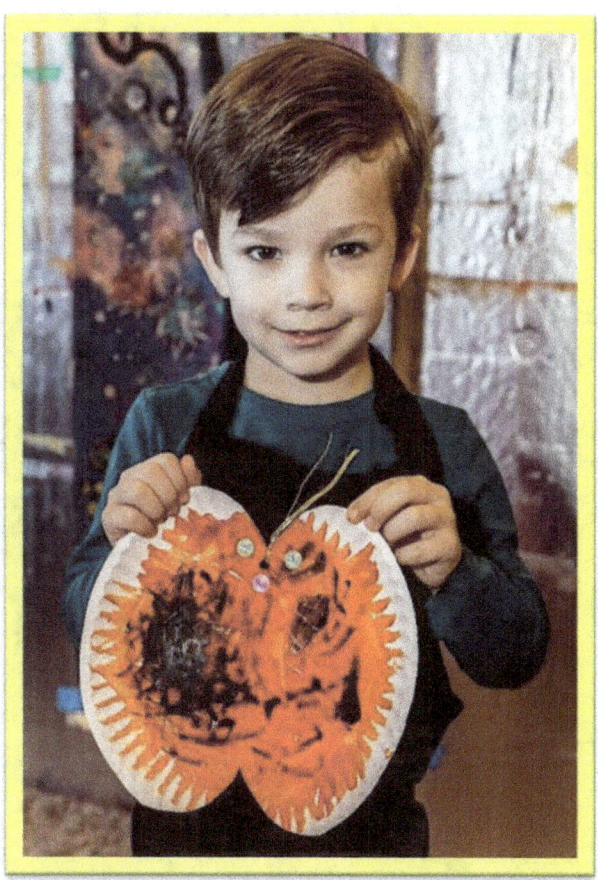

Instructions:

1. Lay out the surface protector.
2. Put a large cookie-sized drop of yellow paint on one side of the paper plate.
3. Put another large cookie-sized drop of red paint on the other side of the plate.
4. Have your child mix the paint together on the paper plate with hands to make orange.
5. After the whole plate is colored in, allow the paint to dry.
6. Use black paint to make the lines with fingers or brush in the Monarch's wings.
7. Once dry, fold the paper plate in half and trim each pointy end into a rounded shape, for wings.
8. You can put a hole punch in the center and put a pipe cleaner or ribbon through to make antennae.

Making real-world connections with an
Accompanying activity, **to reinforce learning and show children how art relates to their daily lives.**

- *You Tube video:*

Monarch butterflies, amazing migration to Mexico.

This short video is both beautiful and educational and sure to capture your child's attention.

Unit #3: Mixing Secondary colors

Activity #6 – Making a Beetle

FOCUS: Mixing Primary colors red and blue to make the Secondary color purple

MATERIALS:
surface protector
paper plate
red paint
blue paint
black construction paper
googly eyes
scissors
stapler
glue

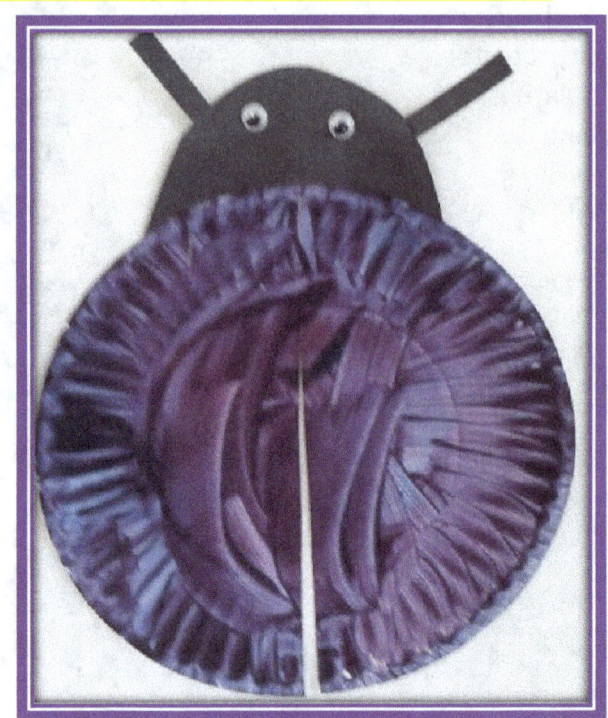

Instructions:

1. Set out paper plate.
2. Put a drop of red paint on one side of the plate.
3. Put a drop of blue paint on the other side of the plate.
4. Have your child mix and blend the paint until it makes purple.
5. Let the plate dry.
6. After the plate dries, fold the plate in half with the purple side out.
7. Cut a slit along the fold, stopping 3 inches from the opposite side of the plate.
8. Cut out a black half circle for the beetle's head.
9. Staple the wings to the beetle's head.
10. Then glue googly eyes onto the head.
11. Cut two small strips of black construction paper for antennae if desired.

Making real-world connections with an
Accompanying activity, to reinforce learning and show children how art relates to their daily lives.

- *You tube video :* **Purple Jewel beetle and giant African fruit beetle.**
This very short video is good for getting a close-up look at the beautiful colors of these two beetles.

Unit #3: Mixing Secondary colors

Activity #7– Making a Grasshopper

FOCUS: Mixing Primary colors blue and yellow to make green

MATERIALS:
surface protector
paper plate
blue paint
yellow paint
green construction paper
green pipe cleaner
stapler
hole punch
googly eyes
glue

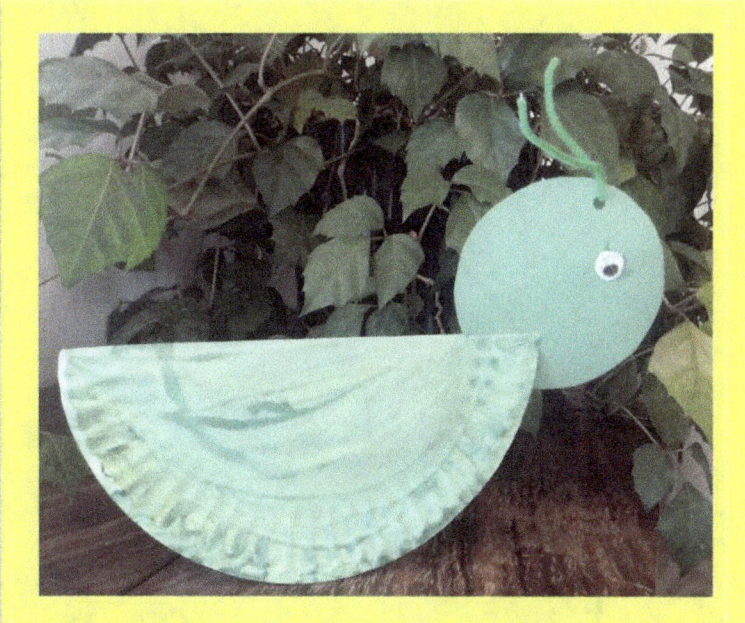

Instructions:

1. Lay out the surface protector.
2. Lay out the paper plate.
3. Put a large drop of yellow paint on the paper plate.
4. Put a large drop of blue paint on the opposite side of the paper plate.
5. Have your child mix the paint with fingers until it turns green and spread it over the paper plate.
6. Allow the paint to dry.
7. Fold the paper plate in half with the green side out for the grasshopper's body.
8. Use the stencil to trace and cut out a circle from the green construction paper for the grasshopper's head.
9. Cut a small slit at the edge of the fold of the body.
10. Place the grasshopper's head into the slit and staple in place.
11. Glue on googly eyes.
12. Punch a hole in the head and string the pipe cleaner through for antennae.

Making real-world connections with an
Accompanying activity, **to reinforce learning and show children how art relates to their daily lives.**

- **You tube video: Planet Earth Amateur Edition grasshopper.**
  This short video gives a great close-up view of a grasshopper climbing a tree.

Grasshopper Head Template

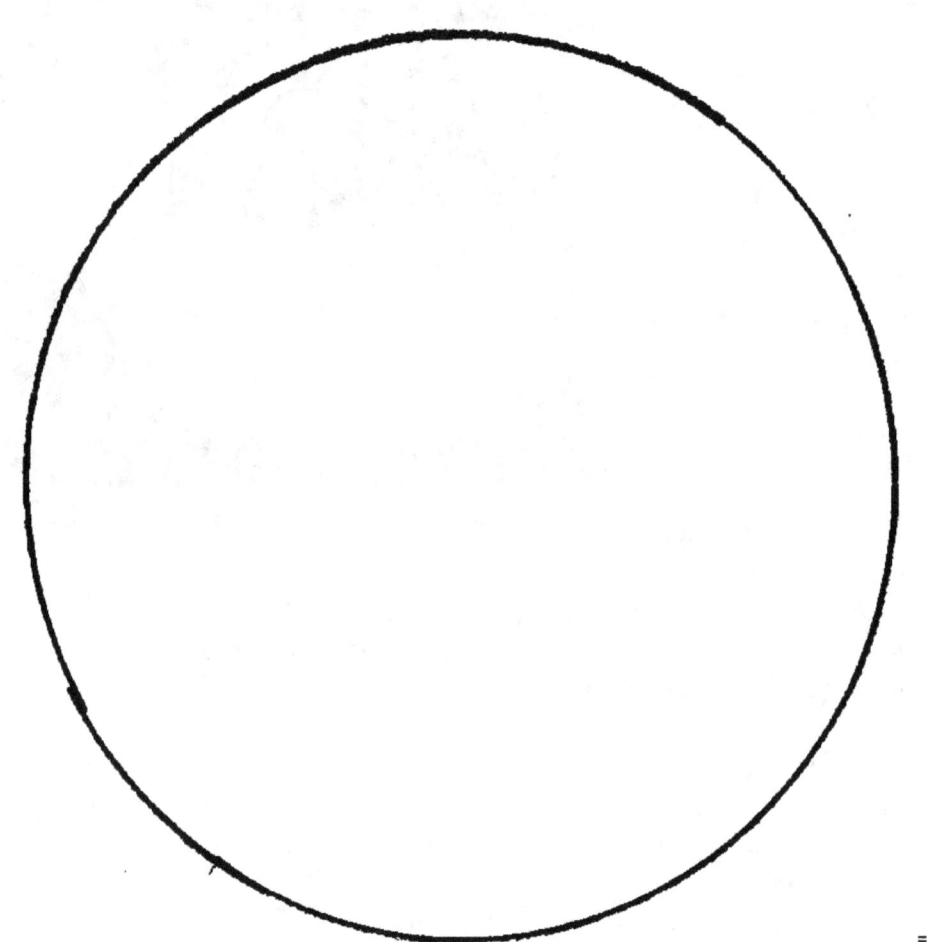

Unit #3: Mixing Secondary colors

Activity #8- Freezing and melting colored glaciers
(Can be separated into three separate activities)

FOCUS: Mixing the Secondary colors

MATERIALS:
water
6 sandwich sized zip lock bags
red food color
blue food color
yellow food color
3 large white plastic dishpans

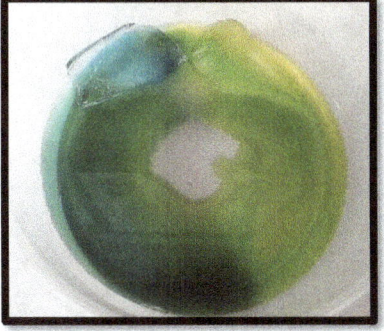
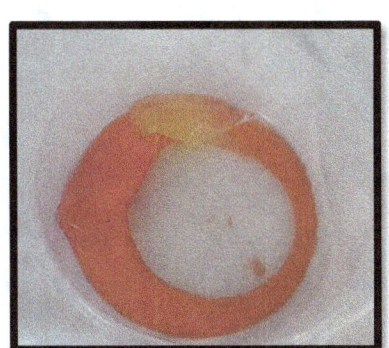
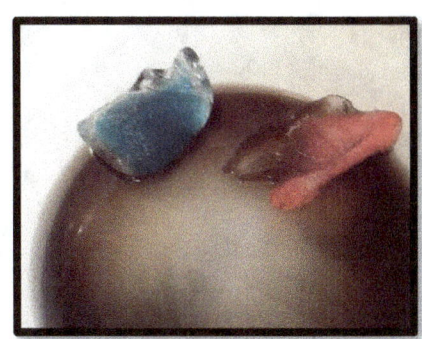

Instructions:

1. Fill 6 sandwich size zip-lock baggies with one cup of water each.
2. Add 4 drops of red food coloring to two of the bags.
3. Add 4 drops of blue food coloring to two of the bags.
4. Add 4 drops of yellow food coloring to two of the bags.
5. Zip up the bags and place in the freezer.
6. Allow bags to freeze solid overnight.
7. Once the ice is frozen, cut two bags open at a time in the following order:
   (Melting these two bags of Primary colors together will make the Secondary colors.)
8. Place one yellow and one blue glacier bag into the same dishpan together and allow to melt to make green.
9. Place one yellow and one red glacier bag into another dishpan together and allow to melt to make orange.
10. Place one red and one blue glacier bag into another dishpan and let it to melt to make purple.

Making real-world connections with an
Accompanying activity, **to reinforce learning and show children how art relates to their daily lives.**

- *Reading:* (Book) **Glaciers: Nature's Icy Caps**

Unit Four: Painting with fingers & objects
Introduction and explanation

The focus is on basic skills as we review the Primary colors red, blue and yellow *and* mixing the Secondary colors green, orange and purple. As you reinforce the names of the Primary and Secondary colors, children will simultaneously be learning to manipulate paint with their fingers, hands, and Q-tips. Activities in this unit provide fine motor skill exercises.

Encourage your child to repeat the vocabulary words as you talk about each activity.

Vocabulary

Red	Green
Blue	Orange
Yellow	Purple
Fingerprint	Thumb print
Spider	Frog
Lion	Flamingo
Flower	

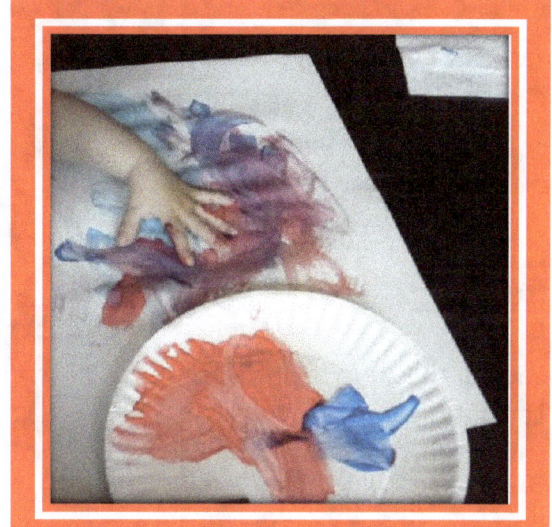

Learning styles addressed
Visual
Kinesthetic - Fine motor

Learning connections
Art- colors:
  red,
  blue,
  yellow,
  green,
  orange,
  purple

Physical activity: manipulation of paint

Science: animals and their habitats; plants and their environments.

Unit #4: Painting with fingers & other objects

Activity #1 – Using fingers to mix the tint light blue

> **FOCUS:** mixing blue and white to make light blue

MATERIALS:
surface protector
sheet of paper
paper plate
blue paint
white paint

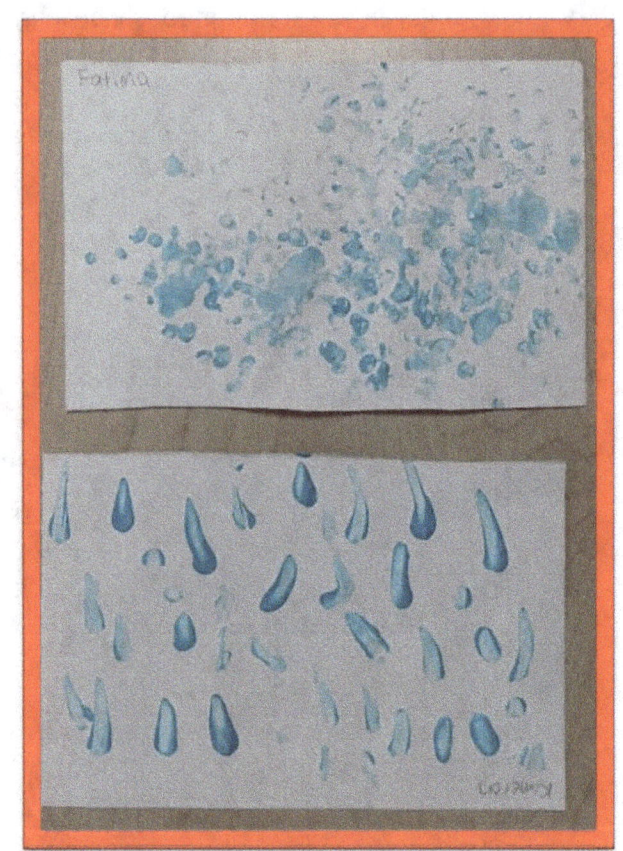

Instructions:

1. Lay out the surface protector.
2. Lay out the paper.
3. Lay out the paper plate.
4. Put a large drop of white paint on the paper plate.
5. Put a smaller drop of blue paint on the other side of the plate.
6. Have your child mix the blue and white paint together with fingers.
7. Once a light blue is achieved, use fingers to put dots on the paper to make rain drops.
8. You have created a rainy-day scene!

Making real-world connections with an
Accompanying activity, **to reinforce learning and show children how art relates to their daily lives.**

- *Activity:* **Take a walk outside and notice the color of the sky. Is it dark blue or light blue?**

Unit #4: Painting with fingers & other objects

Activity #2 – Making a Creepy spider

FOCUS: Finger painting

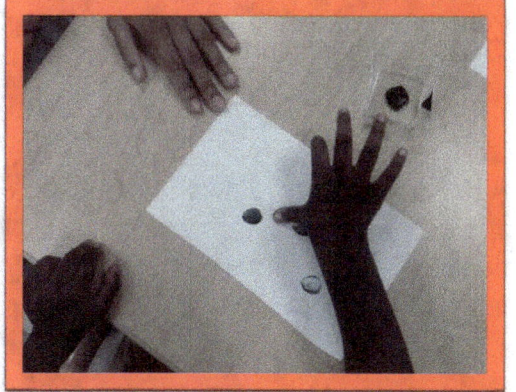

MATERIALS:
surface protector
sheet of paper
paper plate
black paint
fine tip black Sharpie marker

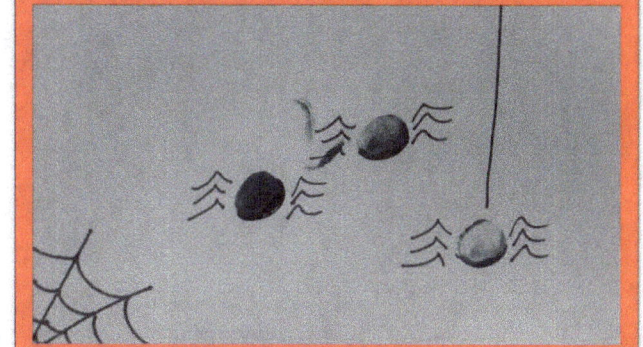

Instructions:

1. Lay out the surface protector.
2. Lay out the paper.
3. Lay out the paper plate.
4. Put some black paint on the paper plate.
5. Dip the child's thumb into the black paint.
6. Place the child's thumb onto the paper and press to form a fingerprint.
7. Use the black Sharpie to make lines next to the thumbprint to create spider legs.
8. Draw a line from the spider's head to the top of the page, like the spider is hanging from its web.

Making real-world connections with an
Accompanying activity, to reinforce learning and show children how art relates to their daily lives.

- *Movie:* Charlotte's web. Talk about the good spider.

Unit #4: Painting with fingers & other objects

Activity #3- Making a hoppy frog

> **FOCUS:** Finger painting

> **MATERIALS:**
> construction paper
> green paint
> fine tip black Sharpie marker

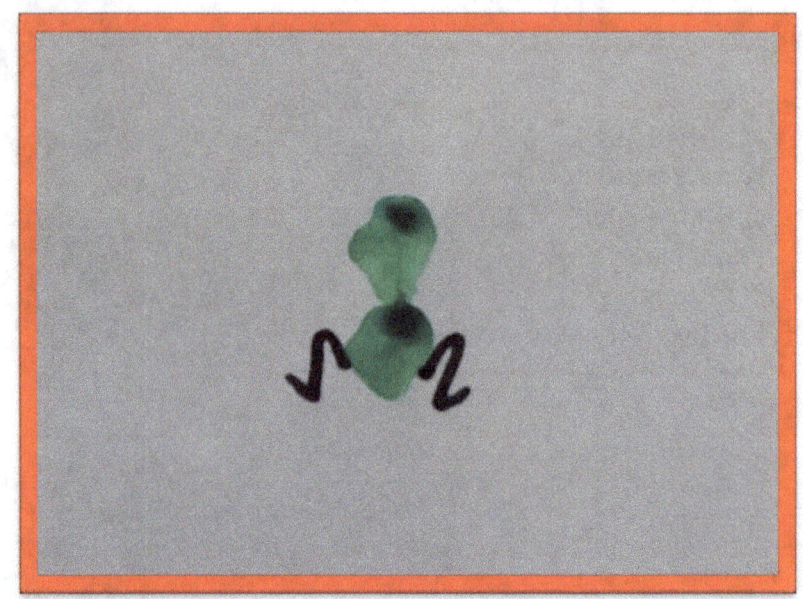

Instructions:

1. Lay out the surface protector.
2. Lay out the paper.
3. Put some green paint on the paper plate.
4. Dip your child's thumb into the green paint.
5. Place your child's thumb onto the paper and press to form a fingerprint.
6. Dip the child's thumb into the paint again and place the second fingerprint on top of the first fingerprint.
7. You now have the head and body of the frog.
8. Have your child use the sharpie to make eyes and legs.

Making real-world connections with an
Accompanying activity, to reinforce learning and show children how art relates to their daily lives.

- *Activity:* **Take a walk in the park by the pond. See if you can find frogs jumping.**

Unit #4: Painting with fingers & other objects

Activity #4- Making a happy Butterfly

MATERIALS:
surface protector
sheet of paper
paper plate
paint (color of choice)

FOCUS: Finger painting

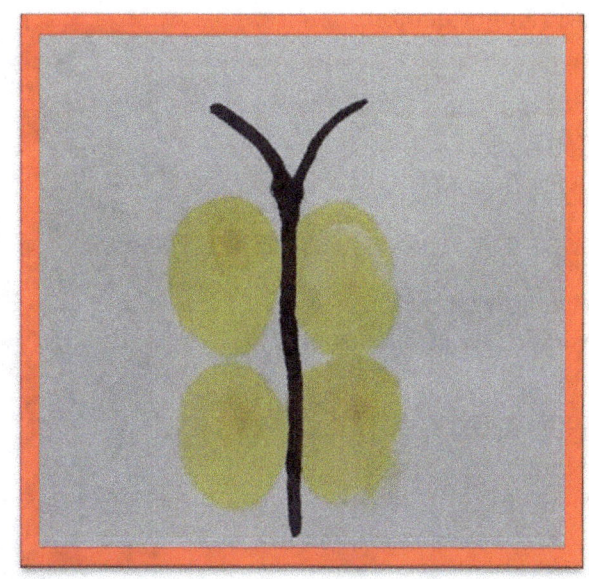

Instructions:

1. Lay out the surface protector.
2. Lay out the sheet of paper.
3. Lay out the paper plate.
4. Place a large drop of paint on the paper plate.
5. Dip your child's thumb into the paint.
6. Place your child's thumb on the paper and press to form a fingerprint.
7. Dip your child's thumb into the paint again.
8. Place thumb on paper and press to form a fingerprint directly under the first fingerprint.
9. Dip child's thumb into paint.
10. Place your child's thumb on the paper and press to form a fingerprint directly next to the first fingerprint.
11. Dip your child's thumb into the paint again.
12. Place your child's thumb onto the paper and press to form a fingerprint directly next to the second fingerprint.
13. Now you have the butterfly's wings.
14. Draw a line between the butterfly's wings with the Sharpie to create the body.
15. Then use the Sharpie to draw antennae.

Making real-world connections with an
Accompanying activity, **to reinforce learning and show children how art relates to their daily lives.**

- **Activity: Take a walk outside. See if there are any butterflies flying. Can you catch one?**

Unit #4: Painting with fingers & other objects

Activity #5- Making a smiling lion

FOCUS: Finger painting

MATERIALS:
surface protector
paper plate
glue stick
pre-cut yellow circle that
  fits inside circle of paper plate
pre-cut black triangle for nose
two pre-cut circles for eyes
brown paint
black sharpie

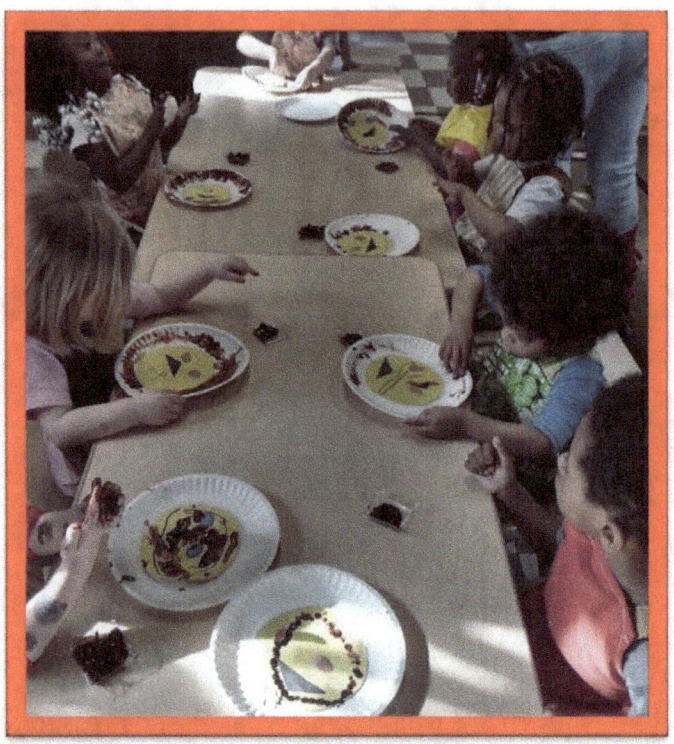

Instructions:

1. Lay out the surface protector.
2. Lay out the paper plate.
3. Use the glue stick to glue the yellow circle on the paper plate for the lion's face.
4. Use the glue stick to glue the eyes on the lion's face.
5. Use the glue stick to glue the triangle onto the lion's face for the nose.
6. Use the black Sharpie marker to draw on the lion's mouth.
7. Finger paint with brown around the lion's face to make the lion's mane.

Making real-world connections with an
Accompanying activity, to reinforce learning and show children how art relates to their daily lives.

- *Activity:* Go to your local zoo. Find the lions. Can you hear them roar?
- *Reading:* Book: Peek-A-Boo Zoo

Unit #4: Painting with fingers & other objects

Activity #6 - Making a spring flower

FOCUS: Finger painting

MATERIALS:
surface protector
sheet of paper
paper plate
red paint
yellow paint

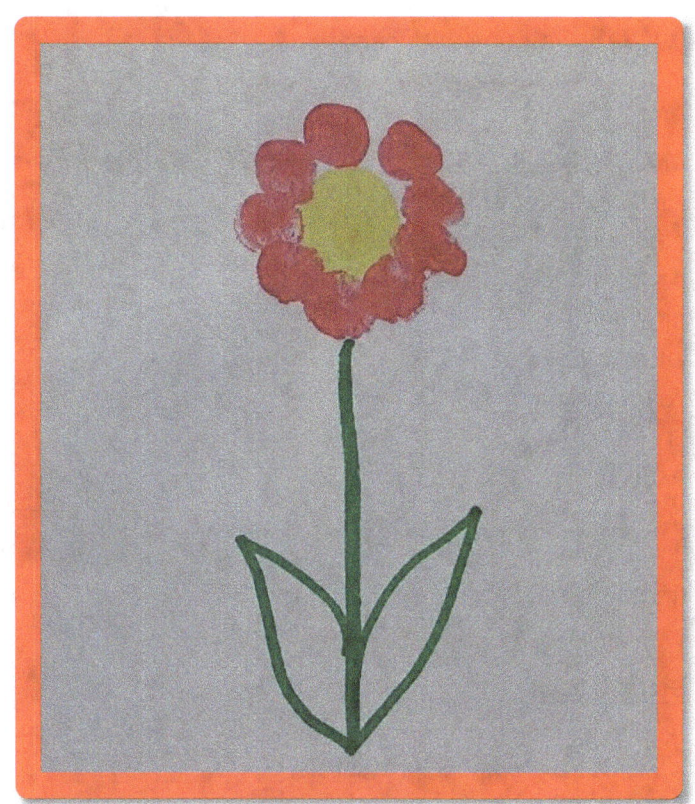

Instructions:

1. Lay out the surface protector.
2. Lay out the sheet of paper.
3. Lay out the paper plate.
4. Put a large drop of yellow paint on the paper plate.
5. Dip your child's thumb into the yellow paint.
6. Make a thumbprint for the center of the flower.
7. Put a large drop of red paint on the paper plate.
8. Dip your child's index fingers into the red paint and make fingerprints around the center for petals.
9. Draw a stem with the sharpie.

Making real-world connections with an
Accompanying activity, to reinforce learning and show children how art relates to their daily lives.

- *Activity:* It's springtime! Choose a pretty flower and plant it in a pot or in the flower bed.

Unit #4: Painting with fingers & other objects

Activity #7 - Making a colorful Flamingo

FOCUS: Painting with hands

MATERIALS:
surface protector
blue construction paper
paper plates
pink paint
white paint
yellow paint
green paint
paint brush
googly eyes
liquid glue
fine tip black Sharpie marker

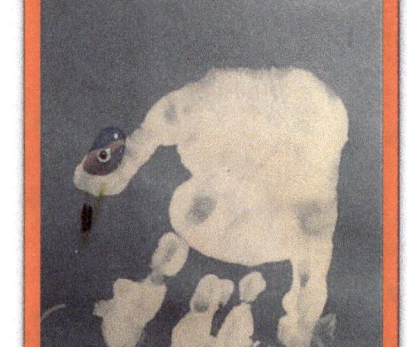

Instructions:

1. Lay out the surface protector.
2. Lay out the blue construction paper.
3. Lay out the paper plate.
4. Put a large drop of pink paint on a paper plate.
5. Dip your child's hand into the pink paint. (Or paint the hand, as seen above.)
6. Place your child's hand on the paper to make a handprint.
7. Turn the paper upside down.
8. Assist your child to paint the legs and beak on with yellow paint, using the paintbrush.
9. Assist your child with painting on the green grass with a paintbrush.
10. Then, with the white, make some ripples in the water with the paintbrush.
11. Glue on a googly eye.

Making real-world connections with an
Accompanying activity, to reinforce learning and show children how art relates to their daily lives.

- *Activity:* Go to your local zoo. Find the Flamingos

- *Reading:* Book: Peek-A-Boo Zoo

Unit #4: Painting with fingers & other objects

Activity #8- Painting a Primary color Dayscape

FOCUS: Finger painting using Primary colors Colors: red, blue, yellow

MATERIALS:
surface protector
sheet of paper
paper plate
red paint
blue paint
yellow
paint
Q-tips

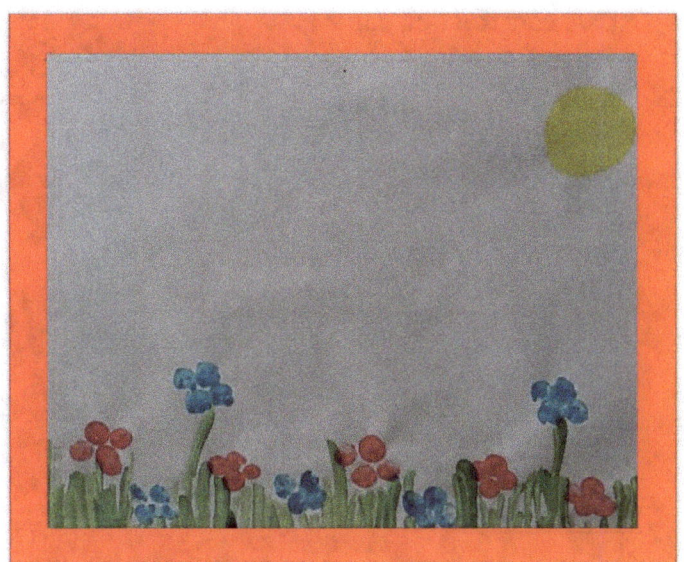

Instructions:

1. Lay out the surface protector.
2. Lay out the sheet of paper.
3. Lay out the paper plate.
4. Place a small drop of red paint on the paper plate.
5. Place a small drop of blue paint on the paper plate.
6. Place a small drop of yellow paint on the paper plate.
7. Have your child finger paint the sun yellow in the top half of the paper.
8. Use red and blue to paint flowers using fingerprints near the bottom of the page.
9. If desired, mix blue and yellow to make green for grass and use Q-tips to paint it on the paper.
10. You have created a dayscape!

Making real-world connections with an
Accompanying activity, **to reinforce learning and show children how art relates to their daily lives.**

- *Reading:* **Book: Where is Little Fish**

Unit #4: Painting with fingers & other objects

Activity #9 - Ocean scene

FOCUS: Mixing Primary colors to make Secondary colors

MATERIALS:
surface protector
blue construction paper
red paint
yellow paint
white paint
googly eyes
glue
fine tip black Sharpie marker

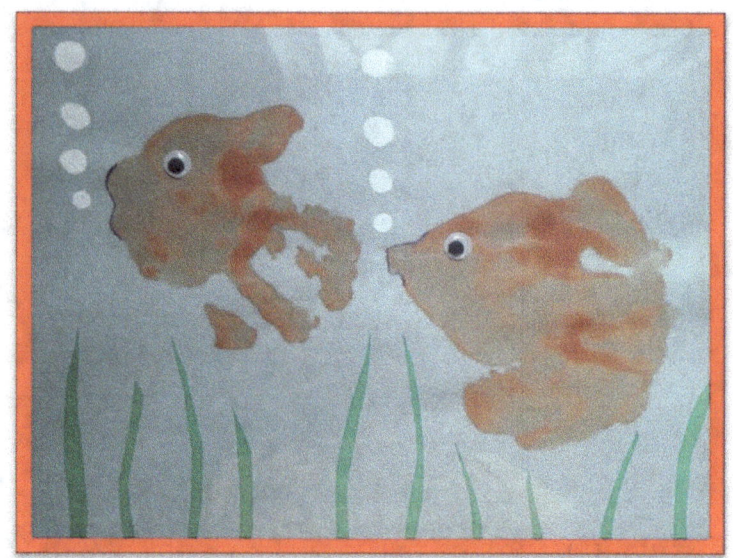

Instructions:

1. Lay out the surface protector.
2. Lay out the blue construction paper.
3. Mix red and yellow paint to make orange for the fish.
4. With the paintbrush, paint your child's hand orange.
5. Place your child's hand on the blue paper to make a handprint.
6. After the fish have dried, glue on googly eyes for the fish eyes.
7. Draw on mouths with the Sharpie.
8. Dip pointer finger into the white paint and make bubbles coming from the fish mouths.

*Optional: cut thin strips of green construction paper and glue to the bottom of the paper for seaweed.

Making real-world connections with an
Accompanying activity, to reinforce learning and show children how art relates to their daily lives.

- *Reading:* Book: **Where is Little Fish**

Unit Five: Painting with the brush
Introduction and explanation

The focus is on basic skills as children advance from painting with fingers and hands to manipulating a paint brush. In addition to learning to manipulate the paint brush, children will learn to recognize patterns. The patterns stripes and spots are introduced. Activities in this unit provide fine motor skill exercises.

Encourage your child to repeat the vocabulary words as you talk about each activity.

Vocabulary
Red
Purple
White
Brown
Black
Pattern
Stripes

Learning styles addressed
Visual
Kinesthetic - Fine motor

Learning connections
Art- colors: red, purple,
        black, white, brown
        Pattern: stripes, spots

Physical activity:
manipulation of paintbrush

Science: animals and insects

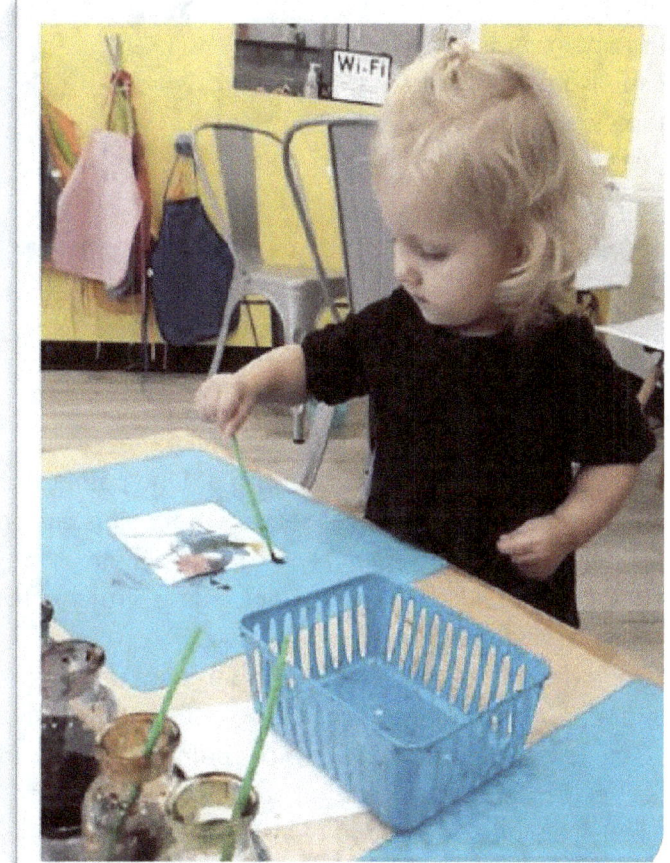

Unit #5: Painting with the brush

Activity #1 - Purple Emperor butterfly

FOCUS:
painting with the brush

MATERIALS:
surface protector
paper plate
red paint
blue paint
large paint brush
2 small paint brushes
googly eyes
glue
black pipe cleaner
scissors

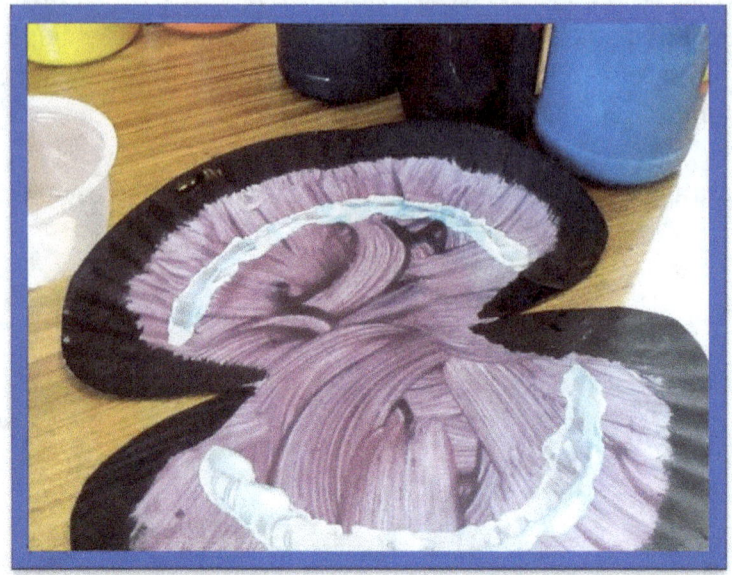

Instructions:

1. Lay out the surface protector and the paper plate.
2. Put a drop of red paint and a drop of blue paint on the paper plate on opposite sides.
3. Have your child mix the paints together using the large brush.
4. Allow the plate 5-10 minutes to dry, explaining that you are waiting for the paint to dry.
5. Have your child blow on the paper plate with you to speed drying (this will keep your child from getting bored).
6. Once the paint is dry, fold the paper plate in half with the colored side facing out.
7. Round off the pointed ends of the paper plate with scissors to form butterfly wings.
8. Use a small paintbrush with black paint to go around the edges of the wings.
9. When finished with the wing outline, use a small brush with white paint to brush a white stripe on the wings.
10. Allow to dry.
11. When finished, glue googly eyes on the butterfly.
12. Use a black pipe cleaner to make antennae. (*Optional)

Making real-world connections with an
Accompanying activity, to reinforce learning and show children how art relates to their daily lives.

- *Reading:* Book: Mr. Peanuckle's Bug Alphabet

Unit #5: Painting with the brush.

Activity #2 – Spotted Lady bug

FOCUS
Painting with the brush

MATERIALS:
surface protector
two paper plates
black construction paper
red paint
black paint
large paintbrush
small paintbrush
glue
googly eyes

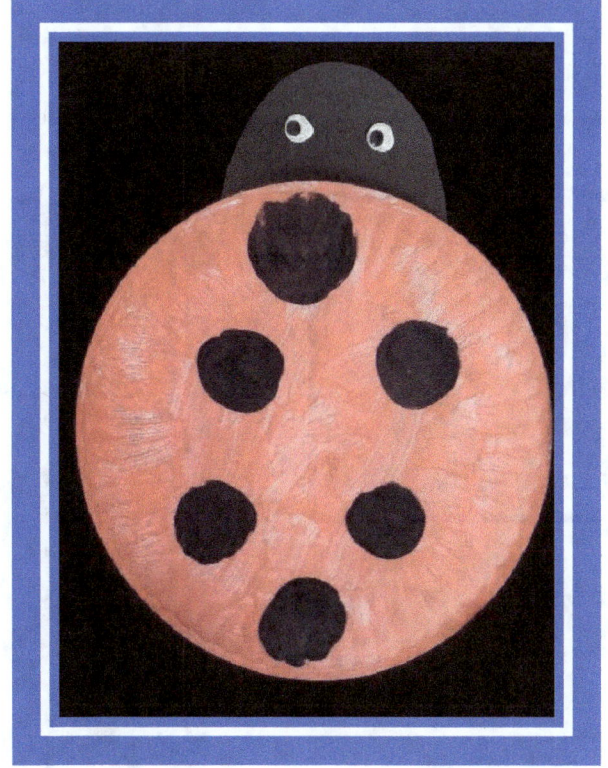

Instructions:

1. Put a drop of red paint on one paper plate.
2. Have your child paint the whole paper plate red, using a paint brush.
3. Put a drop of black paint on another paper plate.
4. Using the small brush, dip the brush into the black paint.
5. Have your child make dots on the red paper plate with the paintbrush to create ladybug spots.
6. Cut out a circle for the head from the black construction paper.
7. Glue the head to the paper plate.
8. Next, you can glue on googly eyes.
9. You can use black pipe cleaners for antennae. (*optional)

Making real-world connections with an
Accompanying activity, to reinforce learning and show children how art relates to their daily lives.

- *Reading:* Book: Mr. Peanuckle's Bug Alphabet

Unit #5: Painting with the brush.

Activity #3 – Painting a zebra

FOCUS
Painting a pattern using the brush

MATERIALS:
surface protector
white construction paper
paper plate
black paint
paint brush
picture of a zebra

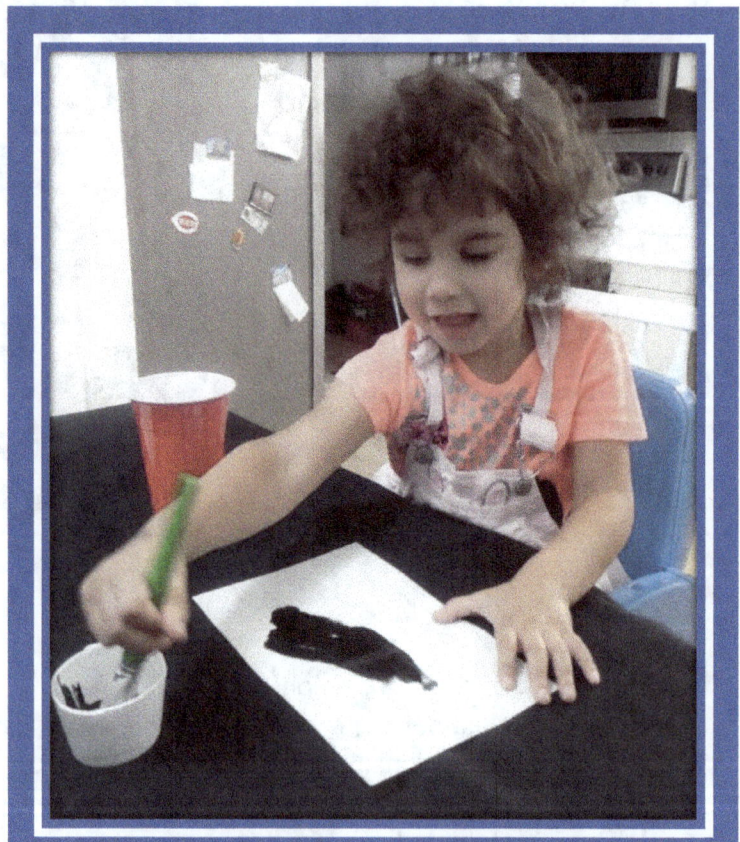

Instructions:

1. Lay out the surface protector.
2. Lay out the white sheet of paper.
3. Show your child some pictures of a zebra.
4. Discuss the stripes on the zebra.
5. Have your child make black stripes on the white paper with the paint brush to make zebra stripes.

Making real-world connections with an
Accompanying activity, **to reinforce learning and show children how art relates to their daily lives.**
• *Reading:* **Book: Peek-A-Boo zoo,** by Jane Cabrera

Unit #5: Painting with the brush

Activity #4 – Painting a Zebra - opposite

> **FOCUS:**
> Painting a pattern with the brush

> **MATERIALS:**
> surface protector
> black construction paper
> paper plates
> white paint
> paint brush
> picture of a zebra

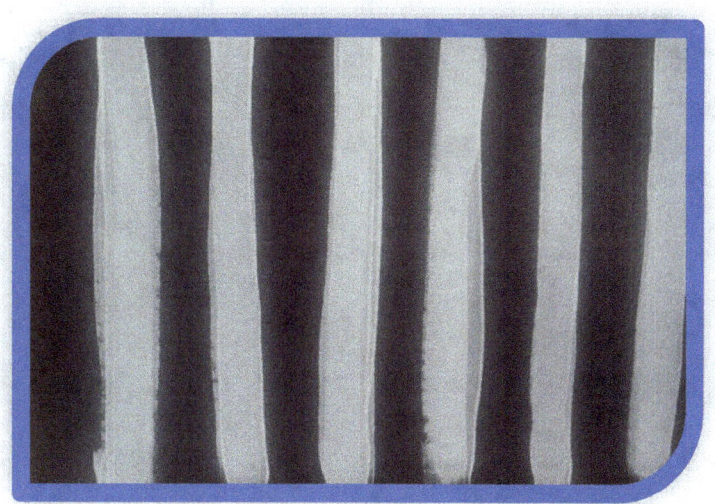

Instructions:

1. Lay out the sheet of black paper.
2. Show your child pictures of a zebra and discuss the picture you made with the black stripes on white paper.
3. Ask your child what would happen if you put white stripes on black paper.
4. Have your child paint white stripes on the black paper like zebra stripes.
5. Just for fun, ask your child if the zebra has white stripes on a black body or black stripes on a white body.

Making real-world connections with an
Accompanying activity, to reinforce learning and show children how art relates to their daily lives.

- *Reading:* Book: **Peek-A-Boo zoo,** by Jane Cabrera

Unit #5: Painting with the brush

Activity #5 -Painting a Giraffe with a brush

> **FOCUS**
> Painting a pattern with the brush

> **MATERIALS:**
> surface protector
> white construction paper
> red construction paper
> orange paint
> brown paint
> paint brushes
> paper towel roll tube
> tape
> scissors
> large googly eyes
> glue
> picture of a giraffe
> giraffe template

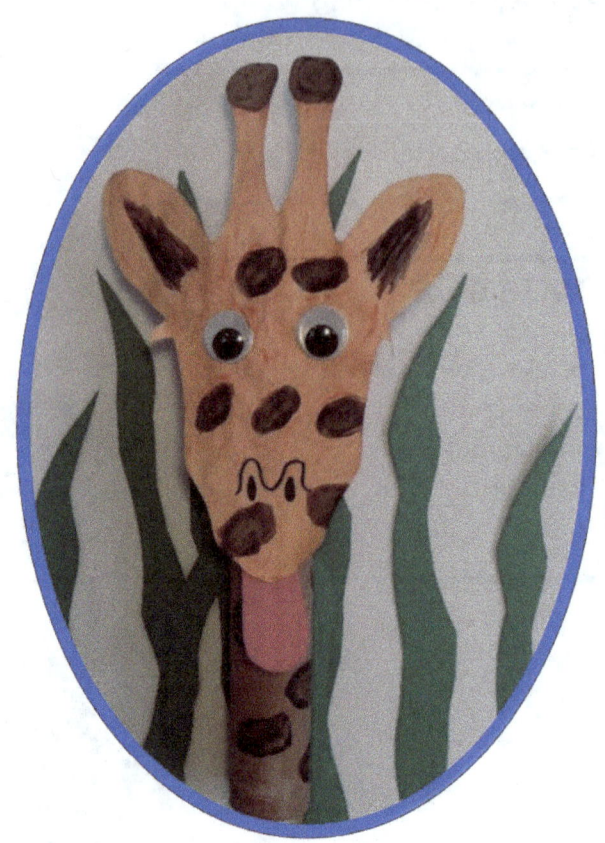

Instructions:

1. Lay out the white sheet of paper.
2. Put a drop of orange paint on a paper plate.
3. Have your child paint this color all over the cardboard tube for the giraffe neck.
4. Trace the template for the giraffe head on the white paper.
5. Using the scissors, cut out the giraffe's head.
6. Have child paint the giraffe's head orange with the brush.
7. Let the tube and head dry.
8. Once dry, glue the googly eyes on.
9. Tape the head to the tube.
10. Now the head is taped to the neck.
11. Using the brush, have your child make spots all over the giraffe with brown paint.
12. Use the sharpie to draw on the nose.
13. Last, cut a strip of red construction paper and tape it to the face for the tongue.

> *Making real-world connections* with an
> *Accompanying activity,* to reinforce learning and show children how art relates to their daily lives.
> • *Reading:* Book: Peek-A-Boo zoo, by Jane Cabrera

Giraffe Template

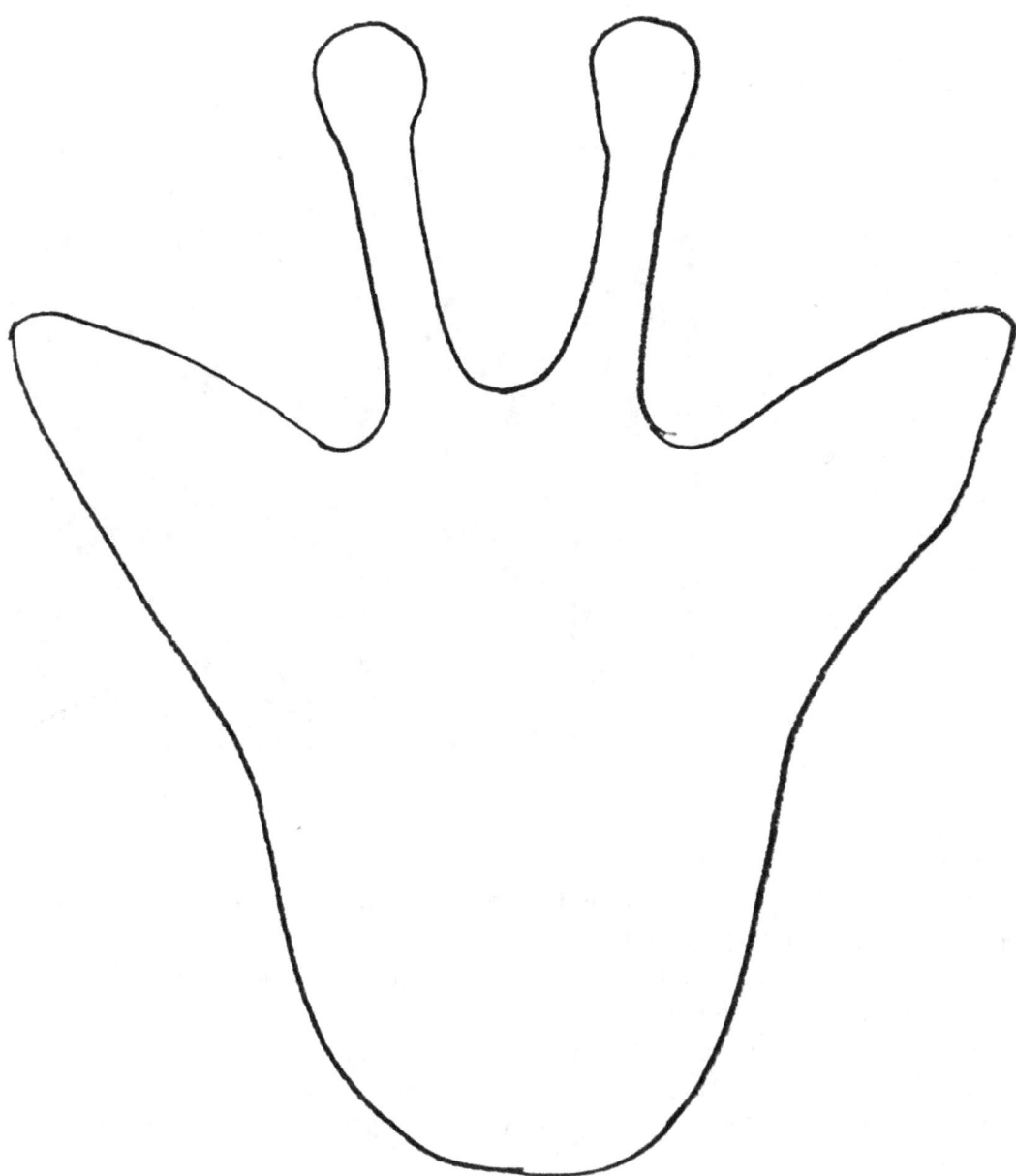

Unit #5: Painting with the brush

Activity #6– Painting a Cheetah pattern

FOCUS:
Painting a pattern with the brush

MATERIALS:
surface protector
white construction paper
paper plates
orange paint
brown paint
black paint
two medium paint brushes
picture of a Cheetah

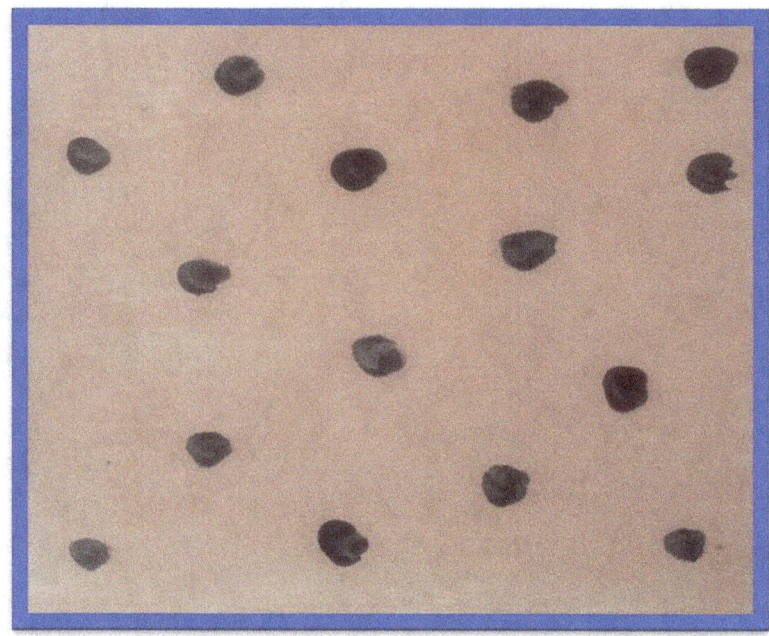

Instructions:

1. Lay out the surface protector.
2. Lay out the sheet of paper.
3. Show your child a picture of a Cheetah.
4. Discuss the picture of the zebra you made and explain that now you are going to paint a Cheetah.
5. Put a drop of orange paint on a paper plate.
6. Have your child use the brush to paint the paper all over with the orange paint.
7. Put a drop of black paint on another paper plate.
8. Put a drop of brown on the same paper plate as the black paint.
9. Have your child mix the black and brown together with the other paint brush.
10. Dip a brush into the mixture of black and brown and make Cheetah spots on the orange paper.

Making real-world connections with an
Accompanying activity, to reinforce learning and show children how art relates to their daily lives.
• *Reading:* **Book: Peek-A-Boo zoo,** by Jane Cabrera

Unit #5: Painting with the brush

Activity #7 – Dalmatian

FOCUS
Painting a pattern with a brush

MATERIALS:
white construction paper
paper plates
black paint
large paintbrush
small paintbrush
pictures of a Dalmation

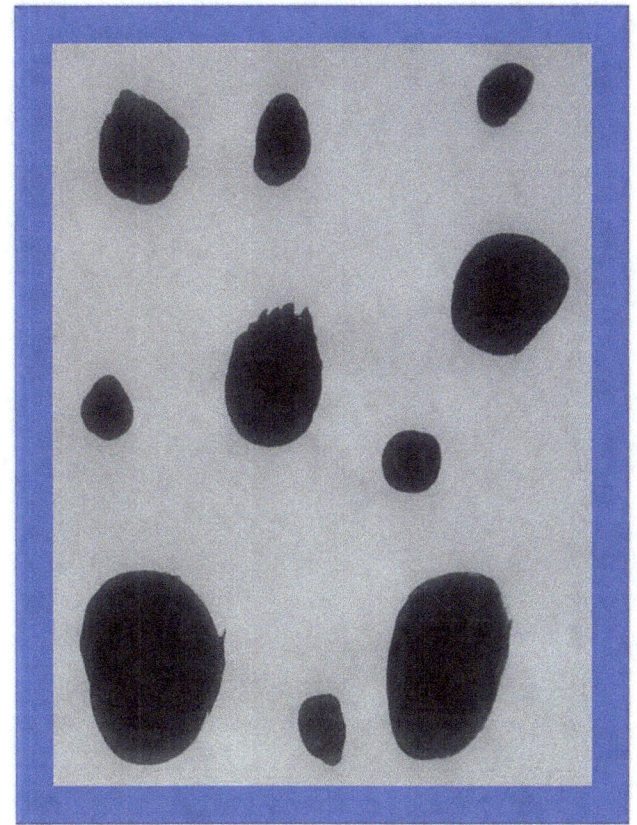

Instructions:

1. Lay out the surface protector.
2. Lay out the sheet of paper.
3. Look at the Dalmatian pictures & discuss the pattern of its fur.
4. Using black paint and different sized brushes, make spots on the white paper to create a Dalmatian pattern

---

Making real-world connections with an
Accompanying activity, to reinforce learning and show children how art relates to their daily lives.

- *Movie:* **101 Dalmations**

Unit six: Drawing

Introduction and explanation

Unit six is experimentation with crayons, sidewalk chalk and large dot markers. Notice the difference in how they feel and the lines they make. Have fun experimenting with colors as you create things in the environment. Activities in this unit provide fine motor skill exercises.

Encourage your child to repeat the vocabulary words as you talk about each activity.

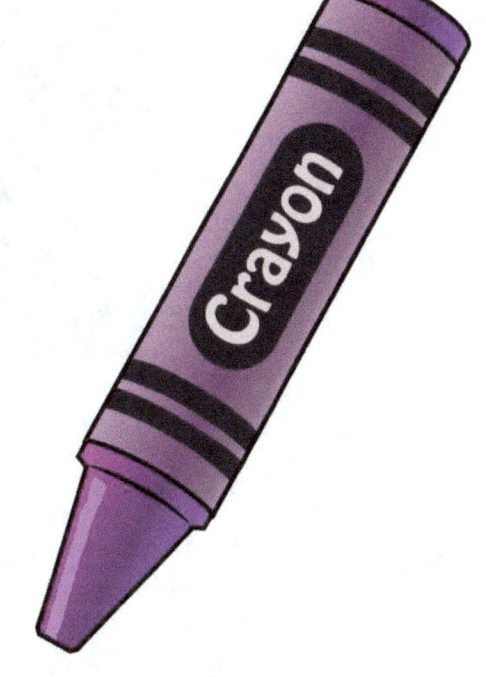

Vocabulary

Family	Animal
Rhinoceros	Starfish
Beach	Sand
Draw	Trace
Dots	

Learning styles addressed

Visual

Kinesthetic - Fine motor

Learning connections

Art- drawing, tracing, coloring

Science- animals and their habitats

Sociology- families and their similarities and differences

Unit #6: Drawing

Activity #1 – Drawing a family

FOCUS:
Drawing with a crayon

MATERIALS:
Surface protector
construction paper
assorted Crayons

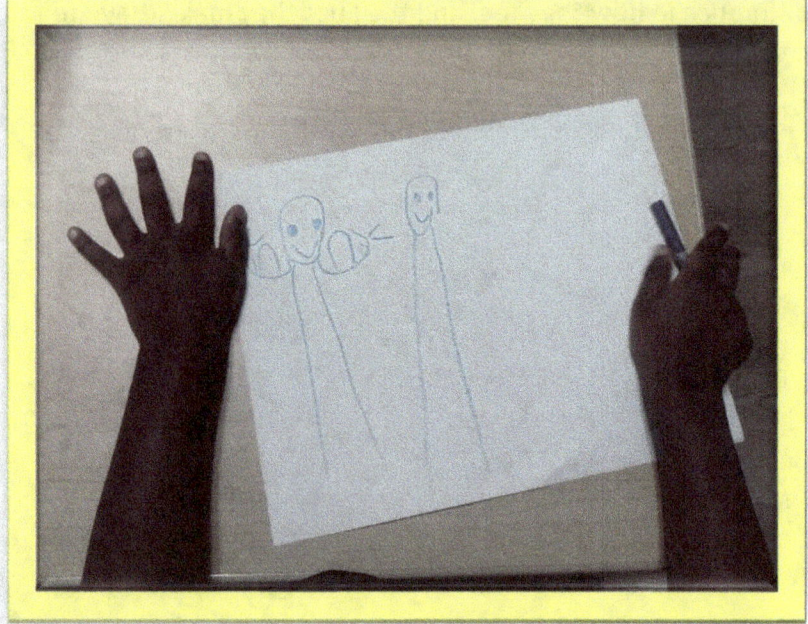

Instructions:

1. Lay out the surface protector.
2. Lay out the construction paper.
3. Lay out the crayons.
4. Talk to your child about the members of your family and notice that some families are different. Some families have mommies and daddies. Some families have grandmas living with them.
5. Tell your child that today you are going to draw a family using crayons.
6. Have your child draw members of the family, freely expressing what family looks like in the child's eyes.

Making real-world connections with an
Accompanying activity, **to reinforce learning and show children how art relates to their daily lives.**

- *Activity:* **Talk about the people in your family. Do you have a traditional or non-traditional family? What do the people in your family look like?**

- *Reading:* **Book: Last stop on Market street,** by Matt de la Pina.
  This is a great book about a grandmother and her grandson taking a trip across town. It is illustrated by Christian Robinson.

Unit #6: Drawing

Activity #2- Drawing an animal

FOCUS:
Drawing with a crayon

MATERIALS:
Surface protector
construction paper
assorted crayons

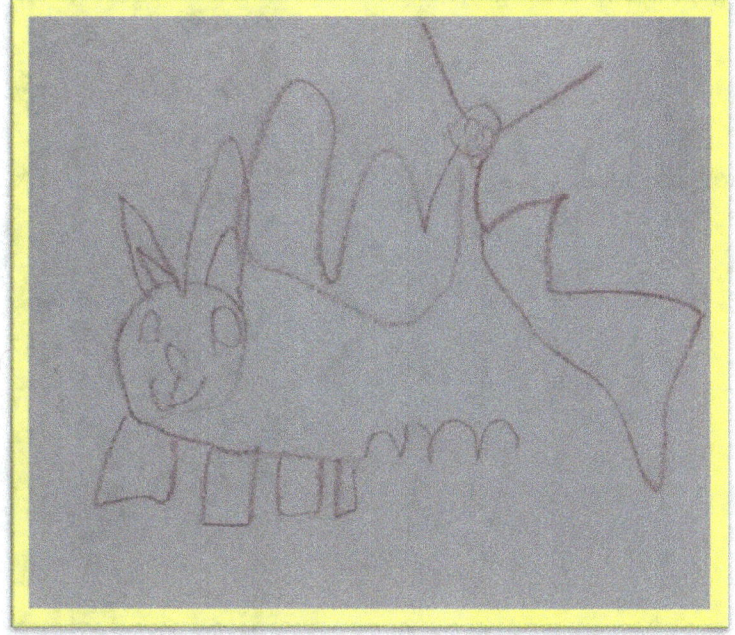

Instructions:

1. Lay out the surface protector.
2. Lay out the paper.
3. Lay out assorted crayons.
4. Talk to your child about pets you have or animals you have seen at the zoo or on t.v.
5. Tell your child that today you are going to draw a picture with crayons.
6. Have your child draw a favorite animal.
7. After your child has drawn the animal, ask your child where the animal lives and what it eats.

Making real-world connections with an
Accompanying activity, to reinforce learning and show children how art relates to their daily lives.

- *Activity:* Take a trip to your local zoo. Look at the animals. See how many you can name. What colors are they? What do they eat?
- *Reading:* Book: Are You My Mother? By P.D. Eastman

Unit #6: Drawing

Activity #3 – Drawing with sidewalk chalk

FOCUS:
Drawing with sidewalk chalk

Materials:
Sidewalk chalk
Sidewalk or patio

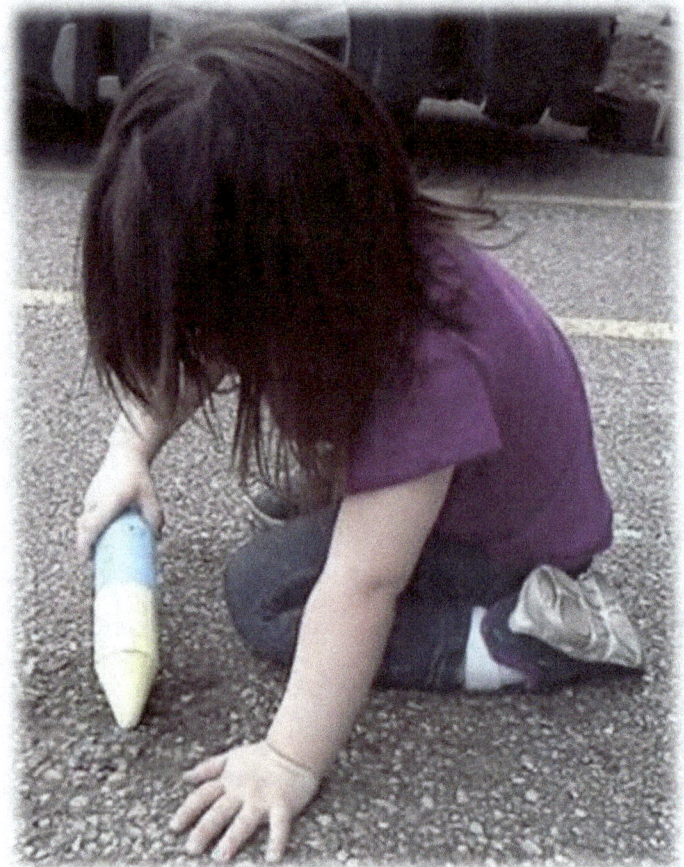

Instructions:

1. Go outside.
2. Give your child the sidewalk chalk.
3. Talk to your child about what you see outside. There are trees and flowers and animals.
4. Ask your child to draw something from the environment.
5. Children love to draw on concrete! Your child may ask you to draw something too!

The collaboration you two come up with will, no doubt, be a beautiful picture and precious time together!

Making real-world connections with an
Accompanying activity, **to reinforce learning and show children how art relates to their daily lives.**

- *You tube video:* **Sidewalk chalk props for Kids Photography**
  This is a cute video that shows children in the artwork. Your child may ask you to create some of these terrific scenes and sit in them!

Unit #6: Drawing

Activity #4 – Starfish handprint

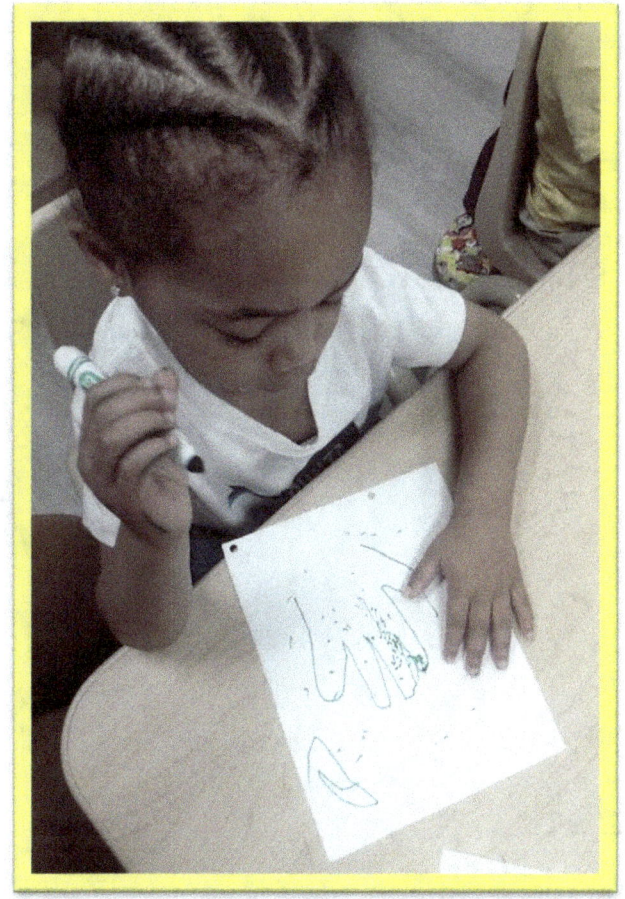

FOCUS: Drawing with crayon

MATERIALS: plain sheet of paper orange crayon assorted crayons

Instructions:

1. Lay out the paper.
2. Lay your child's hand on the paper.
3. Holding your child's hand still, help your child trace it with the orange crayon.
4. After tracing the hand, color or dot it to look like a starfish.
5. Once the starfish is finished, add some ocean plants, sand, or fish!

Making real-world connections with an
Accompanying activity, **to reinforce learning and show children how art relates to their daily lives.**

• *You tube video:* Don Marco

Don Marco shows what can be done using Crayola crayons. I was truly amazed when I first saw his work. His attention to detail is impeccable. His work is something that will make an impression.

Unit #6: Drawing

Activity #5 – Using dot markers

FOCUS:
Using dot markers

MATERIALS:
surface protector
construction paper
favorite color dot marker

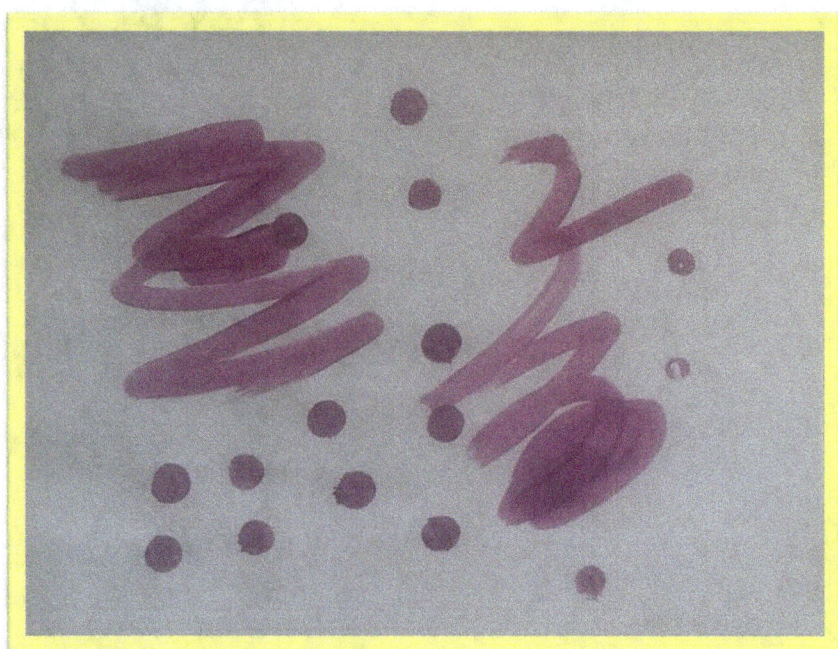

Instructions:

1. Lay out the construction paper.
2. Give your child the marker and have him/ her make any kind of mark.

Using these large markers will give your child the confidence to manipulate objects in the environment.

Making real-world connections with an
Accompanying activity, to reinforce learning and show children how art relates to their daily lives.

- *Activity:* **Notice circles or dots that match the color of your dot marker. Maybe you notice a polka dot pattern on someone's dress, or on wrapping paper.**

Unit #6: Drawing

Activity #6- Making an Octopus

FOCUS:
Using crayons to make shapes

MATERIALS:
construction paper
crayon of choice

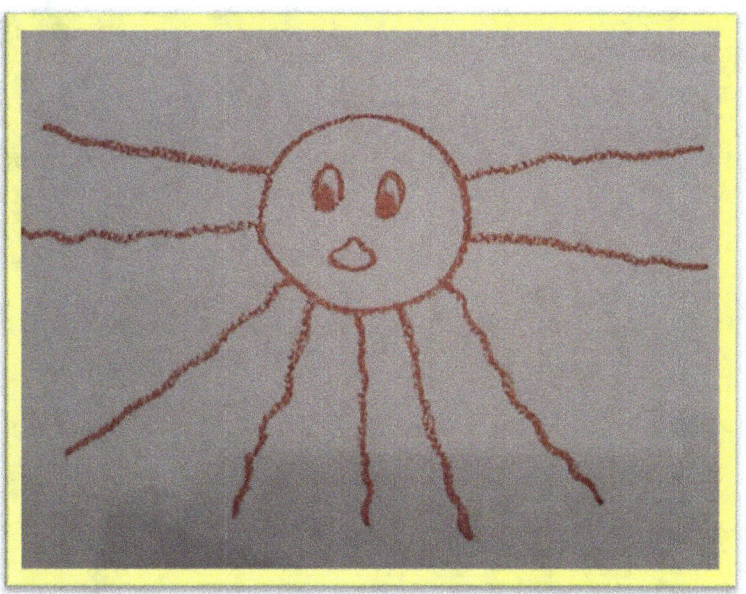

Instructions:

1. Lay out the paper.
2. Help your child make a circle on the paper.
3. Help your child make lines coming out from the circle for the legs of the Octopus.
4. Help your child draw eyes and a mouth for your octopus.

Making real-world connections with an

Accompanying activity, to reinforce learning and show children how art relates to their daily lives.

- *Activity:* **While swimming at the pool, pretend you are an Octopus. You can go into your cave or look for food.**

- *Website:* Etsy

  If you pull up the Etsy website and type in Octopus paintings, you will see a wide variety of Octopi in varied media. I chose this website due to the difficulty in finding an artist who paints only Octopi.

Unit #6: Drawing

Activity #7 - Drawing a beach scene - Feet Fun

FOCUS:
Drawing with crayons

MATERIALS:
construction paper
assorted crayons
assorted markers

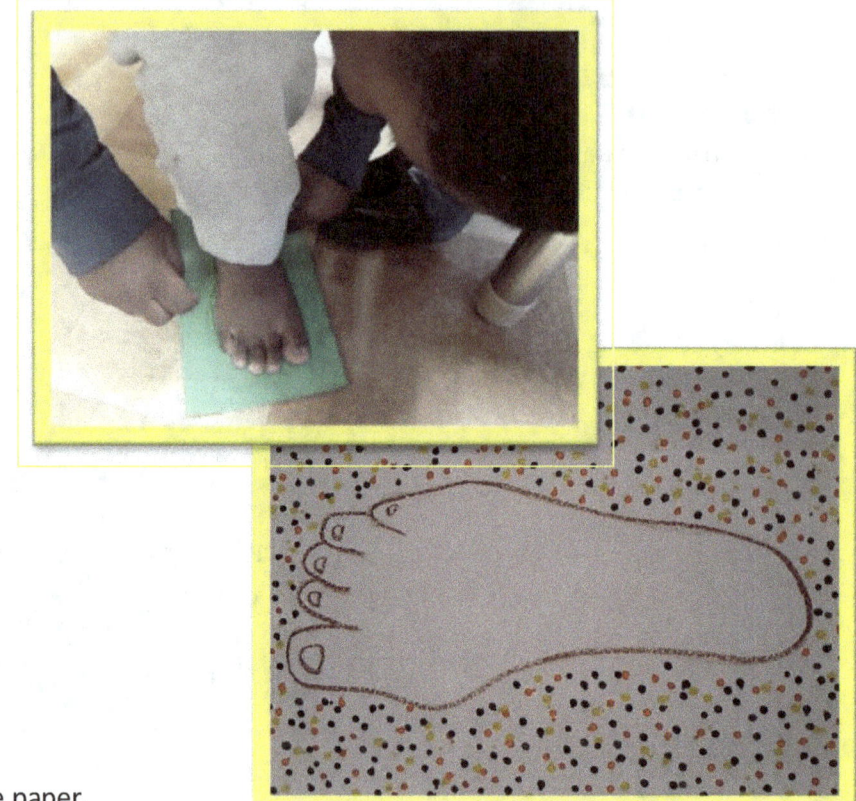

Instructions:

1. Lay out the paper.
2. Have your child stand on the paper.
3. Trace the child's feet with the marker.
4. Let your child use markers to dot all around the footprints to look like sand.
5. Your child can add additional items such as shells, shovel and a pale.

Making real-world connections with an
Accompanying activity, to reinforce learning and show children how art relates to their daily lives.

- *Activity:* **While at the beach, notice your footprints in the sand. Notice the tiny grains of sand. If you can't get to the beach, make footprints with water on the concrete at the pool or on the sidewalk. Notice the little pebbles in the concrete.**
- *Website:* **Kay Crain, Under pool and beach**
  There are many paintings of beach scenes with children and families.

Unit seven: All American Activities
Introduction and explanation

Unit seven looks at traditions of the Fourth of July! Learn about the American flag and get super-sparkly creating your own fireworks! Using a variety of media allows for hours of fun!

Encourage your child to repeat the vocabulary words as you talk about each activity.

Vocabulary
American flag

Stars	stripes
draw	lines
drawing	crayon
paint	painting
red	marker
blue	glue
glitter	fireworks

Learning styles addressed
Visual
Kinesthetic- fine motor

Learning connection
Art- drawing with a
     crayon and a
     marker, painting
     with the brush

American history- American flag

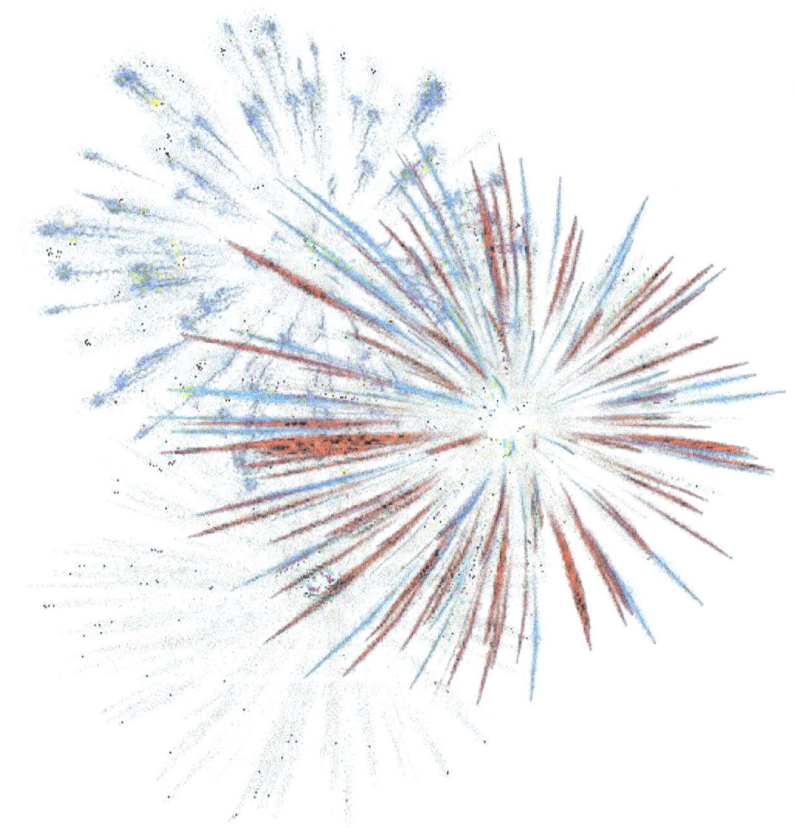

Unit #7: All American activities

Activity # 1 - American Flag

MATERIALS:
surface protector
white construction paper
paper plates
red paint
blue paint
paint brush
white crayon
fine tip black Sharpie marker
wipes

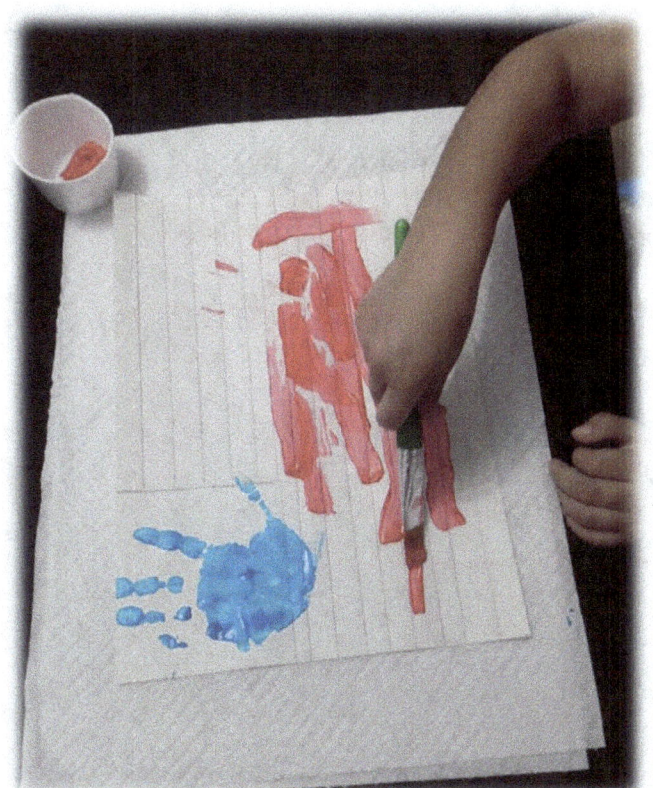

Instructions:

1. Lay out the surface protector.
2. Lay out the sheet of paper.
3. Lay out the paper plates.
4. Using the black marker, draw a square in the upper left corner of the paper.
5. Draw straight lines across the page to make lines for the stripes of the American flag.
6. Put red paint on one paper plate.
7. Put blue paint on another plate.
8. Dip your child's hand into the blue paint.
9. Place your child's hand, with the blue paint on it, inside the square, making a handprint.
10. Clean off your child's hand with the wipes.
11. Dip the brush into the red paint and have your child paint inside every *other* stripe.
12. Once the paint is dry, your child can use the white crayon to draw stars inside the blue handprint.

Making real-world connections with an
Accompanying activity, to reinforce learning and show children how art relates
to their daily lives.

- *Video:* **Chris Pratt Pledge of Allegiance**
  Watch this video and teach your child the Pledge of Allegiance.
- *Video:* **Betsy Ross and the First United States Flag for students, kids**

Unit #7: All American activities

Activity #2 - Creating fireworks

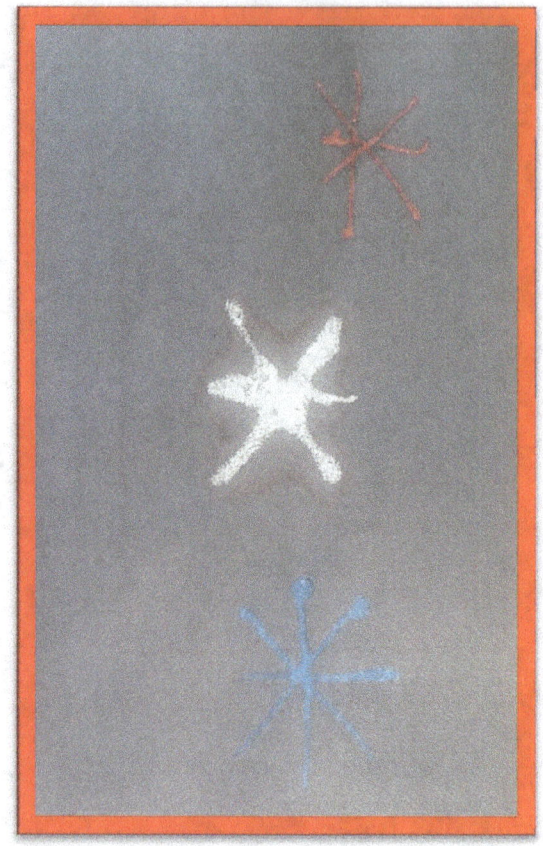

FOCUS:
Manipulating glue
Different effects of glitter on white/colored paper

MATERIALS:
white construction paper
red glitter glue
blue glitter glue
silver glitter glue

Instructions:

1. Lay out the piece of white construction paper.
2. Using the red glitter glue, help your child squeeze it onto the paper to make streaks.
3. Using the blue glitter glue, help your child squeeze it onto the paper to make streaks.
4. Using the silver glitter glue, help your child squeeze it onto the paper to make streaks.
5. You have created a fireworks display!

Making real-world connections with an
Accompanying activity, to reinforce learning and show children how art relates to their daily lives.

- *Activity:* Go outside after its dark and light up your own sparklers.
- *Activity:* Go to see your local fireworks display for the 4th of July.

Unit #7: All American activities

Activity #-3 – Creating fireworks at night

FOCUS:
Manipulating glue.
Different effects of glitter on black

MATERIALS:
surface protector
black construction paper
red glitter glue
blue glitter glue
silver glitter glue

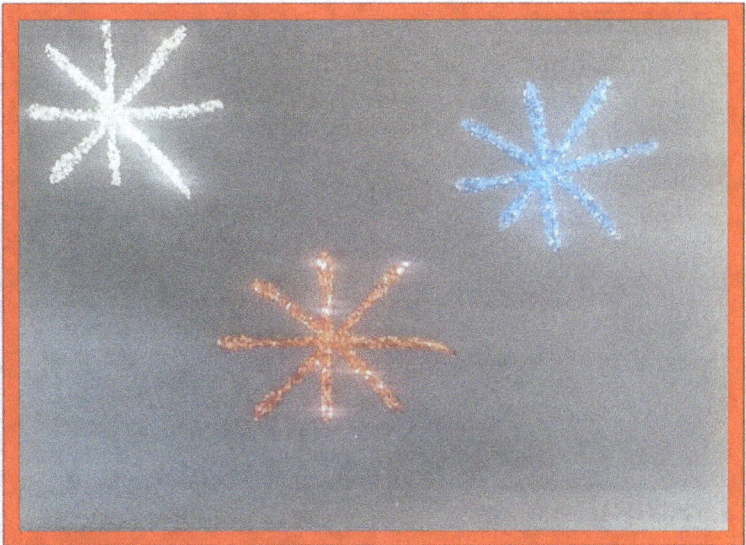

Instructions:

1. Lay out the surface protector.
2. Lay out the black construction paper.
3. Using red glitter glue, help your child squeeze it onto the paper to make streaks.
4. Using blue glitter glue, help your child squeeze it onto the paper to make streaks.
5. Using silver glitter glue, help your child squeeze it onto the paper to make streaks.
6. You have created a nighttime fireworks display!

Making real-world connections with an
Accompanying activity, to reinforce learning and show children how art relates to their daily lives.

- *Activity:* Go to see your local fireworks display for the 4th of July.
- *Reading:* Book: The night before the fourth of July by Natasha Wing

Unit #7: All American activities

Activity #4- Painting fireworks on white

FOCUS:
Creating designs by blowing paint with a straw

MATERIALS:
surface protector
white construction paper
red paint
blue paint
silver paint
straw

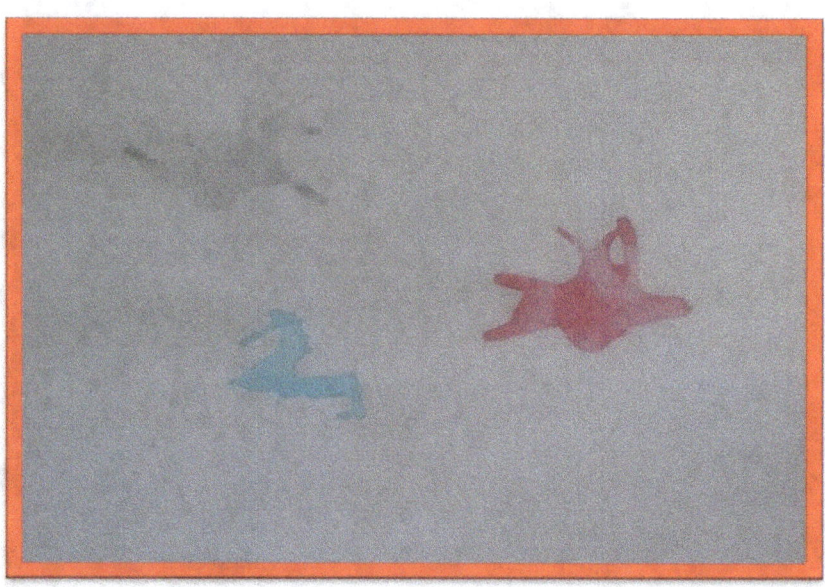

Instructions:

1. Lay out the surface protector.
2. Lay out the sheet of paper.
3. Put a drop of red paint on the white paper.
4. Put a drop of blue paint on the white paper.
5. Put a drop of silver paint on the white paper.
6. Show your child how to move the paint across the paper by blowing it gently through the straw.
7. Have your child blow the paint to make fireworks.
8. You now have a fireworks display!

*Note:
If the paint is too thick to blow, add a little water to it.

Making real-world connections with an
Accompanying activity, to reinforce learning and show children how art relates to their daily lives.

- *Website:* 75 Explosive Photos of Fireworks – Gizmodo
  There are some fantastic photographs here by a variety of artists.

Unit #7: All American activities

Activity #5 - Painting fireworks on black

FOCUS:
Creating designs by blowing paint with a straw

MATERIALS:
surface protector
black construction paper
red paint
blue paint
white paint
straw

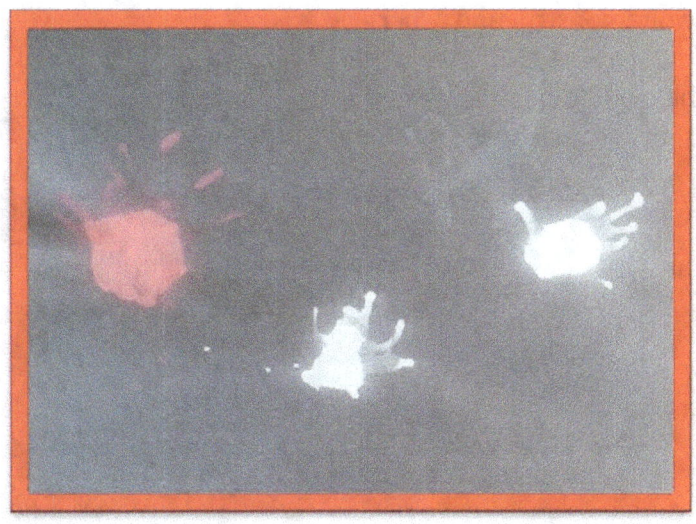

Instructions:

1. Lay out the surface protector.
2. Lay out the sheet of paper.
3. Put a drop of red paint on the black paper.
4. Put a drop of blue paint on the black paper.
5. Put a drop of white paint on the black paper.
6. Show your child how to move the paint across the paper by blowing it gently through the straw.
7. Have your child blow the paint to make fireworks.
8. You now have a nighttime fireworks display!

*Note:
If the paint is too thick to blow, add a little water to it.

Making real-world connections with an
Accompanying activity, **to reinforce learning and show children how art relates to their daily lives.**

- *Website:* **75 Explosive Photos of Fireworks – Gizmodo**

Unit #7: All American activities

Activity #6 - Painting textured fireworks on white

FOCUS:
Creating designs by painting with shaving cream

MATERIALS:
white construction paper
red paint
blue paint
shaving cream

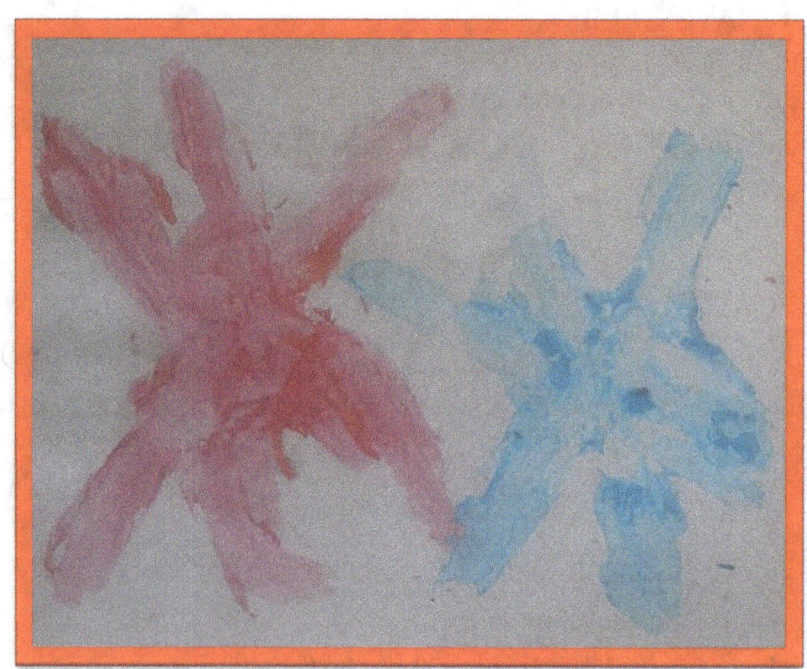

Instructions:

1. Lay out the surface protector.
2. Lay out the sheet of paper.
3. Spray some dots of shaving cream on the paper.
4. Put a little of each color paint on each dot of shaving cream.
5. Have your child create red and blue fireworks by mixing the paint into the shaving cream.
6. Once the shaving cream dries, there will be three dimensional fireworks!

Making real-world connections with an
Accompanying activity, to reinforce learning and show children how art relates to their daily lives.

- *Reading:* Book: Daniel's First Fireworks

Activity #7 - Painting textured fireworks on black

FOCUS:
Creating designs by painting with shaving cream

MATERIALS:
black construction paper
red paint
blue paint
shaving cream

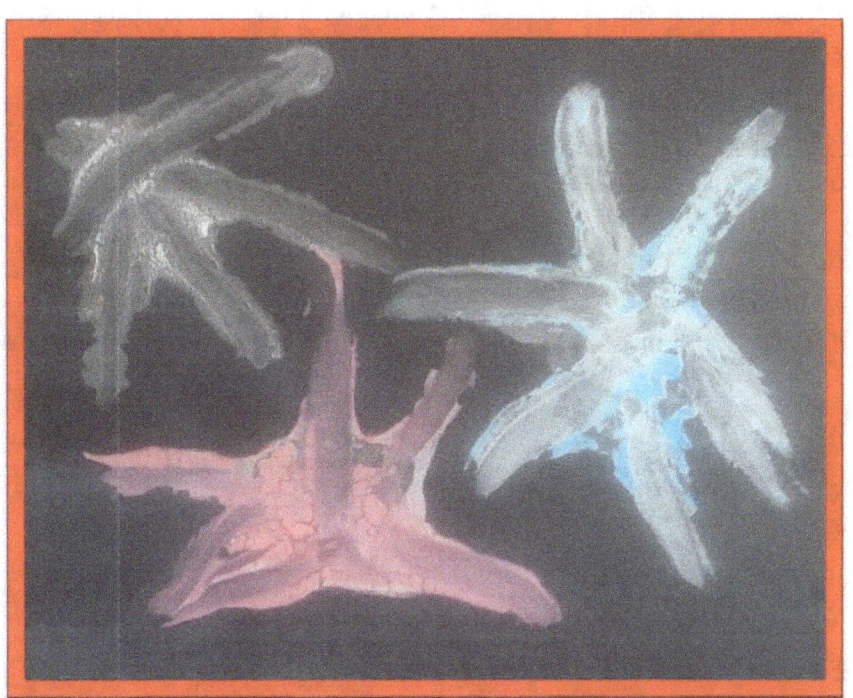

Instructions:

1. Lay out the surface protector.
2. Lay out the sheet of black paper.
3. Spray some dots of shaving cream on the paper.
4. Put a little of each color paint on each dot of shaving cream.
5. Have your child create red, white and blue fireworks by mixing the paint into the shaving cream.
6. Once the shaving cream dries, there will be three-dimensional fireworks at night!

Making real-world connections with an
Accompanying activity, to reinforce learning and show children how art relates to their daily lives.

- *Reading:* Book: Daniel's First Fireworks

Unit eight: Mixed up Miscellaneous
Introduction and explanation

Unit eight is a mixed match of activities. There is experimentation with a variety of media including pottery, sculpture and texture. Hands will get messy and use fine motor skills to feel and manipulate a variety of media! Beading will Introduce coordination skills and dot markers will be used for patterning. Fun will also be had by making bubble paint pictures!

Encourage your child to repeat the vocabulary words as you talk about each activity.

Vocabulary

Ball	bubbles
Roll	blow
Squeeze	design
dot marker	pattern

Primary colors   red   blue
yellow

Learning styles addressed
Visual
Kinesthetic- fine motor, sensory

Learning connections
Art - using playdoh as clay,
        Touching texture,
        recognizing Primary colors
        jewelry making

Math – making patterns

Unit #8: Mixed up miscellaneous

Activity #1 - Introduction to pottery - Making a ball

FOCUS:
Manipulating the shape of Play-Doh

MATERIALS:
surface protector
play-doh

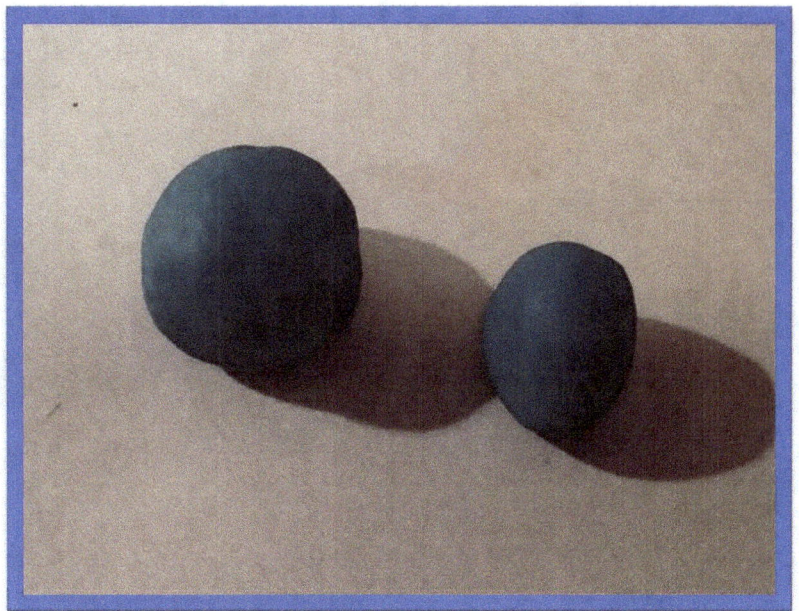

Instructions:

1. Lay out the surface protector.
2. Get a golf ball sized piece of play-doh.
3. Put it between your palms.
4. Squeeze it into as close to a ball shape as you can.
5. Lay the ball on the table and roll it between your palm and table, making it into a ball.
6. Next, get a piece of play-doh between ¼ and ½ the size of your ball.
7. Give it to your child to make a ball.
8. Model how to make a ball again if you need to.

Making real-world connections with an

Accompanying activity, to reinforce learning and show children how art relates to their daily lives.

- *Activity:* **Go to the toy store to see how many different sized balls you can find.**

- *Website:* **Hyakusho**

  On this website, there are photographs of polished clay balls. There are also a couple of very quick videos that show how to form and polish the balls.

Unit #8: Mixed up miscellaneous

Activity #2 - Introduction to sculpture -Making a turtle

FOCUS:
Creating a sculpture by manipulating the shape of Play-doh

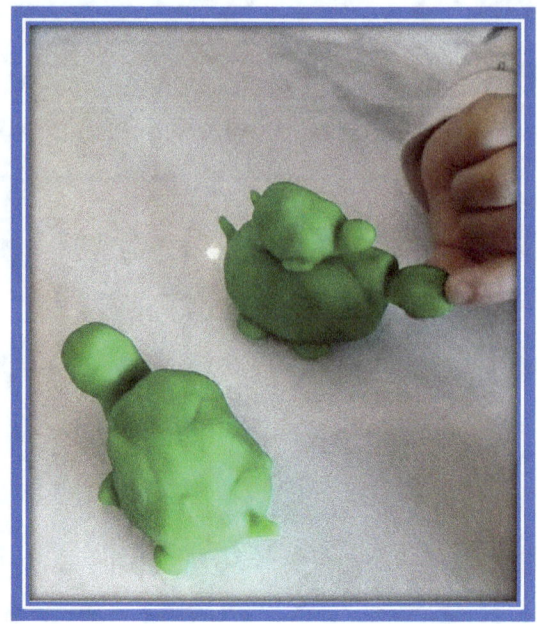

MATERIALS:
Surface protector
Play-doh

Instructions:

Using the skills you just learned to make a ball, you will create a turtle.

1. Lay out the surface protector.
2. Make five pea sized balls by rolling out the play-doh.
3. These will be the turtle's feet and tail.
4. Make one grape sized ball by rolling out the play-doh.
5. This will be the turtle's head.
6. Make one even larger ball, about the size of a jumbo pasta shell, for the turtle's body and shell.
7. Estimate where to put the smaller balls for the feet and tail by laying the body on a surface such as a table.
8. Place the feet and tail on the surface after you have estimated.
9. Help your child place the body on top of the feet and tail and press down so the body sticks.
10. Turn the turtle upside down to attach the head to the front side of the body by gently pressing the head onto the body.

---

*Optional: You can use a pencil to scratch a design into the turtle's shell.

Making real-world connections with an
Accompanying activity, **to reinforce learning and show children how art relates to their daily lives.**

- *Activity:* **Go to the pond on a sunny day. See how many turtles you can count**

Unit #8: Mixed up miscellaneous

Activity #3 - Obleck - introduction to texture

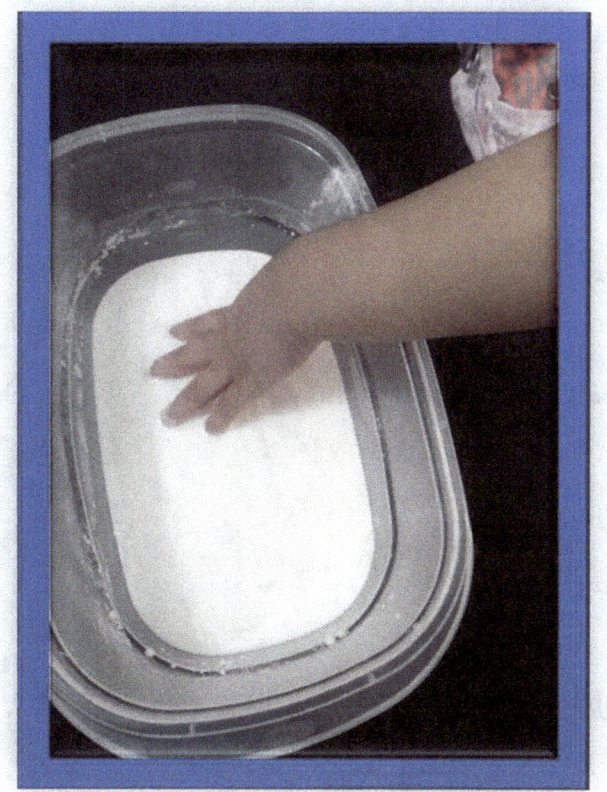

> **FOCUS:**
> Introduction to texture by touch

> **MATERIALS:**
> surface protector
> measuring cup
> 1 Cup cornstarch
> ½ cup water
> disposable aluminum pan
> Food color
> coins

Instructions:

1. Lay out the surface protector.
2. Put the cornstarch in the pan.
3. Add a drop or two of food color. (*optional)
4. Slowly pour the water into the pan, mixing it slowly with the cornstarch.
5. Once the water and cornstarch are mixed, you are ready to experiment with its texture.
6. Have your child feel it, try to pick it up, try to mix it.

Optional:
- Drop a coin into the mixture and watch it sink.
- Try to get it out.

Making real-world connections with an
Accompanying activity, to reinforce learning and show children how art relates to their daily lives.

- *Activity:* **Look for textures in your house and outside that feel different. Try a cotton ball, the rug, the table, the concrete. Is it soft? Is it rough or smooth?**

Unit #8: Mixed up miscellaneous

Activity #4 - Bubble paint design

FOCUS:
Creating a design from bubbles

MATERIALS:
Surface protector
construction paper
bubble mixture for blowing bubbles
food coloring

Instructions:

1. Lay out the surface protector.
2. Lay out the sheet of paper.
3. Place a tablespoon of food color into the bubble bottle.
4. Gently turn the bottle upside down and right side up several times to mix the color.
5. Do this slowly so it won't turn into foam.
6. Have your child blow bubbles through the wand, onto the paper.
7. As the bubbles pop, interesting designs are made!

Making real-world connections with an
Accompanying activity, to reinforce learning and show children how art relates to their daily lives.

- *Activity:* **Go outside and blow bubbles. Watch the wind carry them away!**
- *You tube video:* **This bubble artists amazing bubble skills will blow you away.** This video is fantastic! It shows some amazing things that can be done with bubbles. Both you and your child will be amazed!

Unit #8: Mixed up miscellaneous

Activity #5 – Making a pattern with dot markers

FOCUS:
Reinforcing Primary colors

MATERIALS:
Surface protector
construction paper
red dot marker
blue dot marker
yellow dot marker

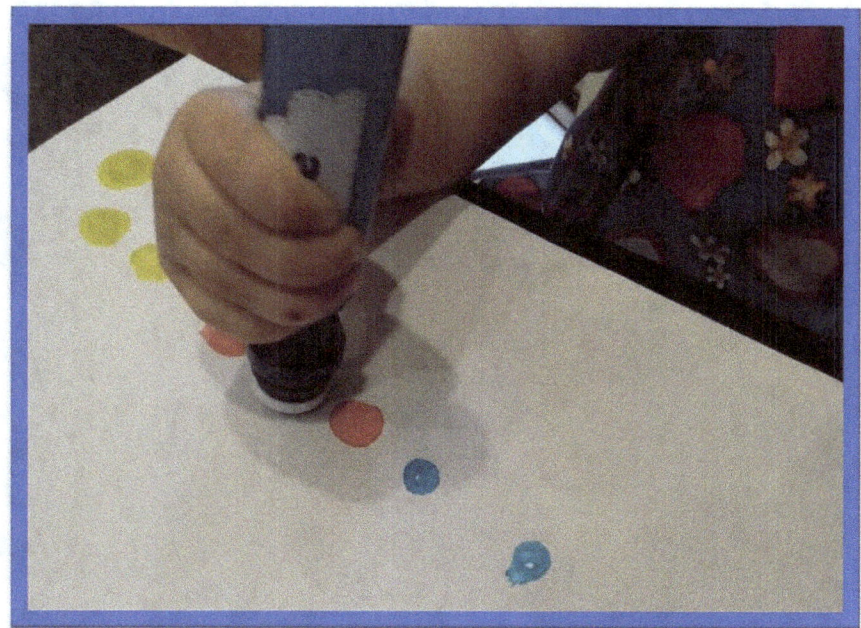

Instructions:

1. Lay out the surface protector.
2. Lay out the sheet of paper.
3. Remind your child of when you used dot markers.
4. Remind your child that red, blue and yellow are Primary colors.
5. Show your child how to make a pattern.
6. Repeat your pattern.
7. Give your child the dot markers and ask your child to make a pattern.
8. Allow your child to come up with his/ her own pattern.

Making real-world connections *with an*
Accompanying activity, **to reinforce learning and show children how art relates to their daily lives.**

- ***Activity:*** **Notice patterns in the environment. Perhaps a restaurant has a checkered tablecloth. Maybe you are wearing a shirt with stripes.**

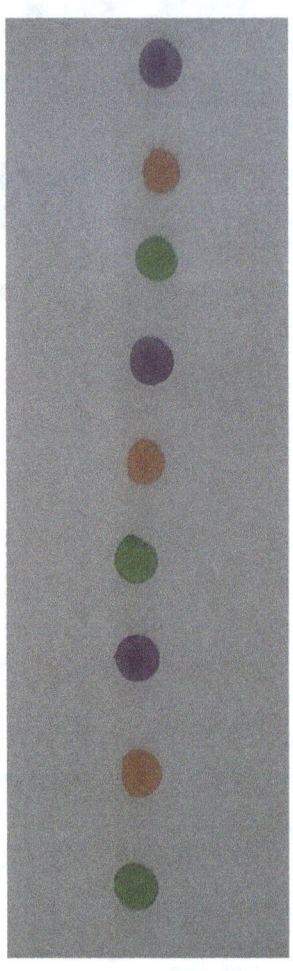

Unit #8: Mixed up miscellaneous

Activity # 6 Dot marker pattern

FOCUS:
Reinforcing Secondary colors

MATERIALS:
surface protector
construction paper
green dot marker
orange dot marker
purple dot marker

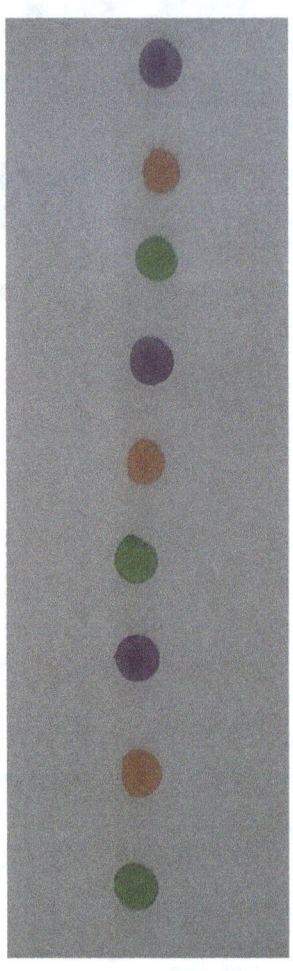

Instructions:

1. Lay out the surface protector.
2. Lay out the sheet of paper.
3. Remind your child that green, orange and purple are Secondary colors.
4. Show your child how to make a pattern.
5. Repeat your pattern.
6. Give your child the markers and ask your child to make a pattern.
7. Allow your child to come up with his/ her own pattern.

Making real-world connections with an
Accompanying activity, to reinforce learning and show children how art relates to their daily lives.

- *Website:* Julia Rothman Illustration and pattern.

Unit #8: Mixed up miscellaneous

Activity #7 – Stringing beads

FOCUS:
stringing beads

MATERIALS:
Surface protector
large pony beads
plastic elastic string
scissors

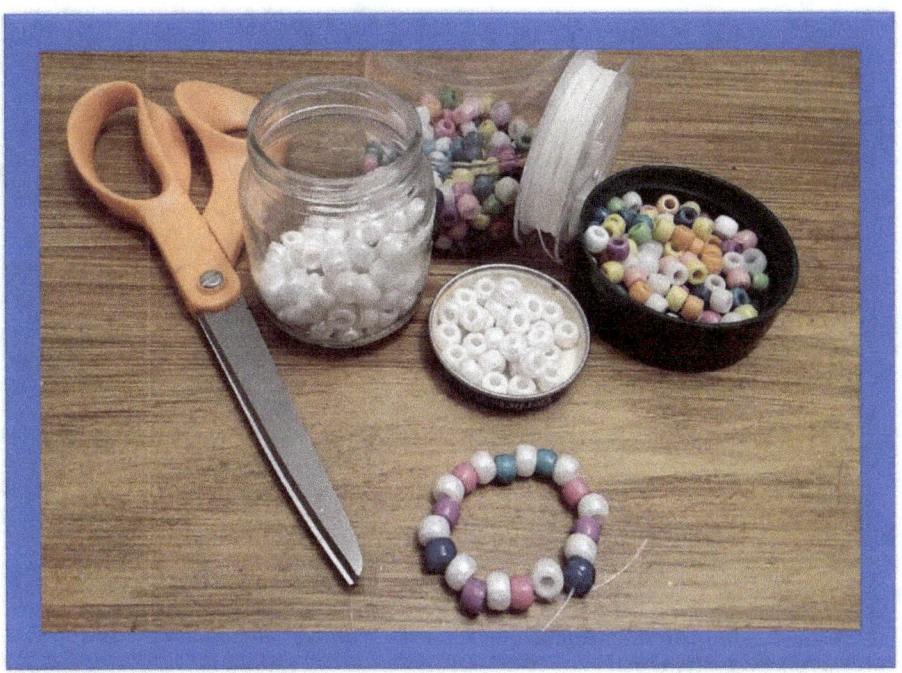

Instructions:

1. Lay out the surface protector.
2. Cut a piece of elastic string.
3. Lay pony beads on the table.
4. Show your child how to put the beads on the string.
5. When the first bead is strung, tie the string around it so it doesn't fall off.
6. Give your child some beads and string and allow your child to string some beads.
7. When the string is large enough to go around the child's wrist, cut and tie it to make a bracelet.

Making real-world connections with an
Accompanying activity, to reinforce learning and show children how art relates to their daily lives.
Activity: **Notice the beaded jewelry at your local art fair.**

Unit #8: Mixed up miscellaneous

Activity #8 – Making a pattern with beads

FOCUS:
patterning with beads

MATERIALS
large pony beads in three colors
plastic elastic string
scissors

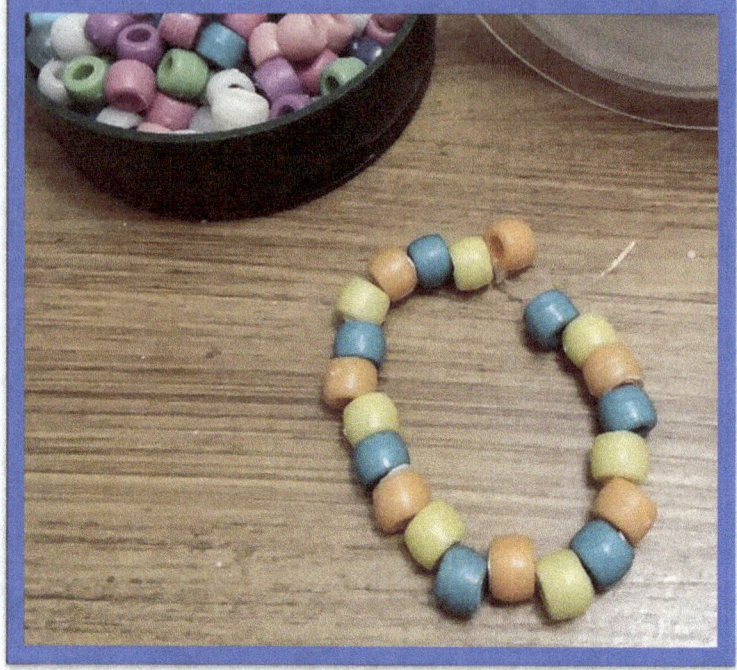

Instructions:

1. Cut a piece of elastic band.
2. Lay the pony beads on the table.
3. String the first bead onto the elastic.
4. When the first bead is strung, tie the string around it so it doesn't fall off.
5. Next, show your child how to make a pattern by putting the beads on the string with one color then the other.
6. Repeat the colors.
7. Give your child some beads and the string and have your child string a pattern.
8. When the string is large enough to go around the child's wrist, cut and tie it to make a bracelet.

Making real-world connections with an
Accompanying activity, to reinforce learning and show children how art relates to their daily lives.

• *You tube video:* KCL The art of making glass beads for jewelry.
This video shows how to fire the actual beads for jewelry making.

Unit nine: Printmaking
Introduction and explanation

Unit nine reintroduces and reinforces the shapes and colors learned in Units One and Two. Printmaking will be explored using the Primary colors red, blue and yellow, along with the shape, circle. The Secondary colors green, orange and purple will also be reintroduced and reinforced as you create more prints! In this unit you will be using a simple circle shape along with a variety of cookie cutters.

Encourage your child to repeat the vocabulary words as you talk about each activity.

Vocabulary

Primary colors   Secondary colors
red   green
blue   orange
yellow   purple
print

Learning styles addressed

Visual
Kinesthetic- fine motor, sensory

Learning connections

Art- colors: red, blue, yellow
        green, orange, purple
        printmaking

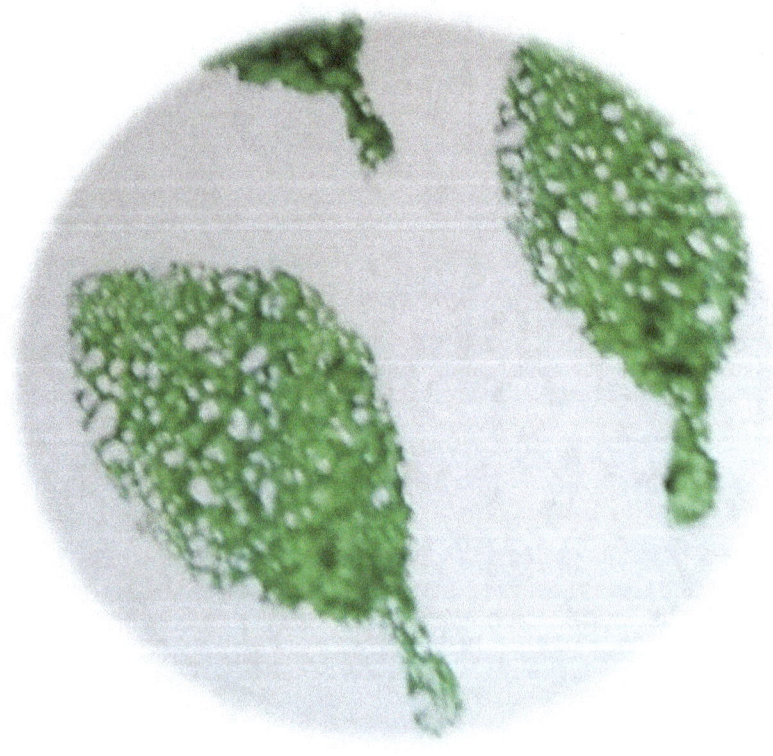

Unit nine: Printmaking

Activity #1 – Making red circles

FOCUS:
Printmaking

MATERIALS:
surface protector
construction paper
paper plates
red paint
styrofoam cup

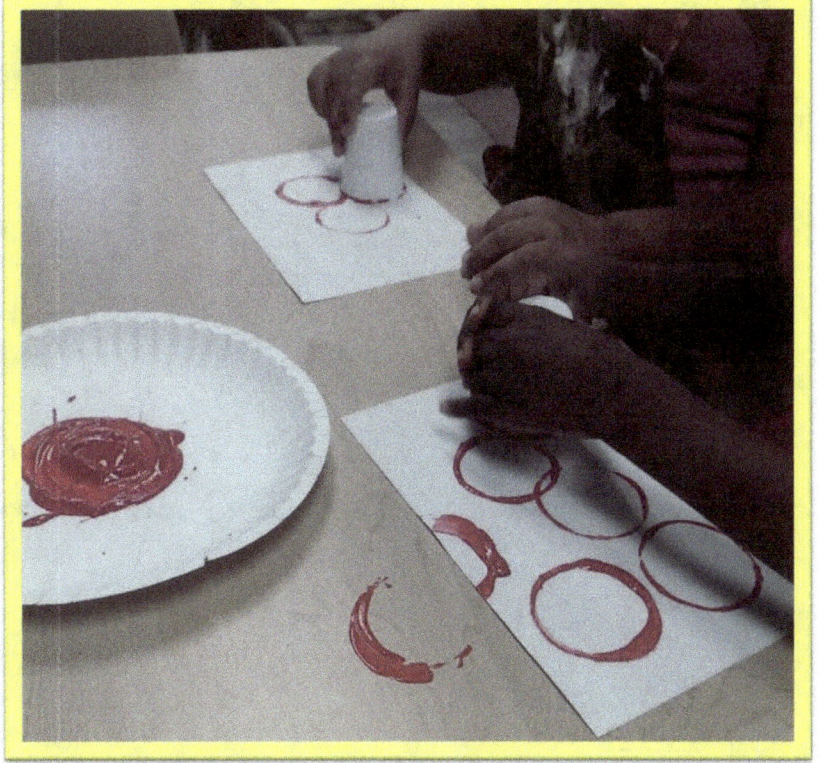

Instructions:

1. Lay out the surface protector.
2. Lay out the sheet of paper.
3. Put a large enough drop of red paint on the paper plate to be the width of the cup.
4. Dip the top of the cup into the red paint.
5. Then, place the cup on the paper to make circles.
6. The circles can be in a row or overlap.

Making real-world connections with an
Accompanying activity, to reinforce learning and show children how art relates to their daily lives.

- *Activity:* Notice things in the environment that are red.
- A stop signis red. What else can you see that's red?

Unit #9: Printmaking

Activity #2 - Making blue circles

FOCUS:
Printmaking

MATERIALS:
surface protector
construction paper
paper plates
blue paint
styrofoam cups

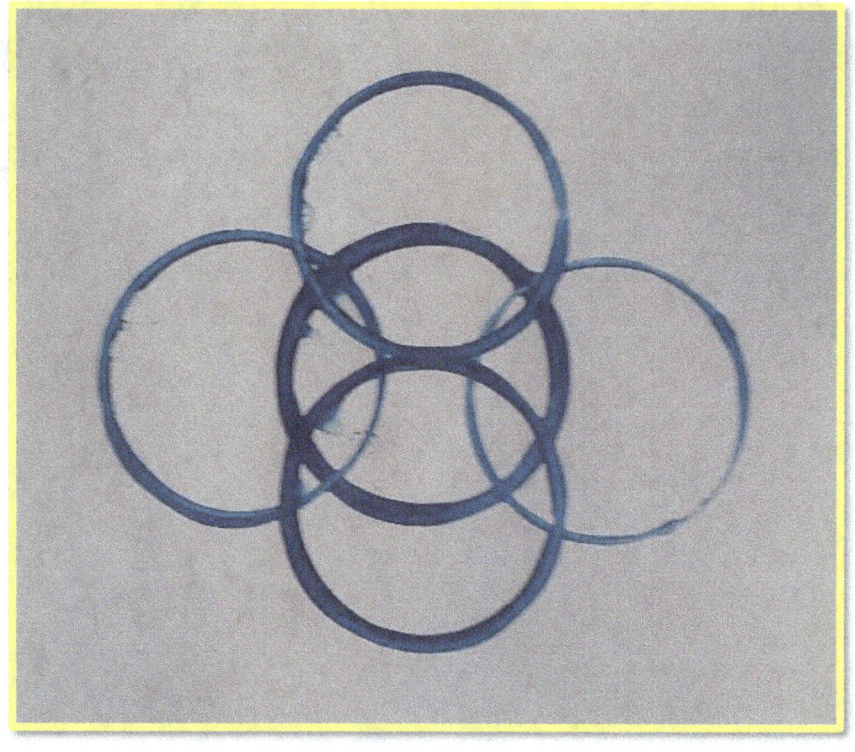

Instructions:

1. Lay out the surface protector.
2. Lay out the sheet of paper.
3. Put a large enough drop of blue paint on a paper plate to be the width of the cup.
4. Dip the top of the cup into the blue paint.
5. Then, place the cup on the paper to make circles.
6. The circles can be in a row or overlap.

Making real-world connections with an
Accompanying activity, to reinforce learning and show children how art relates to their daily lives.

- *Activity:* **Notice things in the environment that are blue. Maybe you can look for blue cars on a trip to the grocery store. Where else can you find something blue?**

Unit #9: Printmaking

Activity #3 - Making yellow circles

FOCUS:
Printmaking

MATERIALS:
surface protector
construction paper
paper plates
yellow paint
styrofoam cup

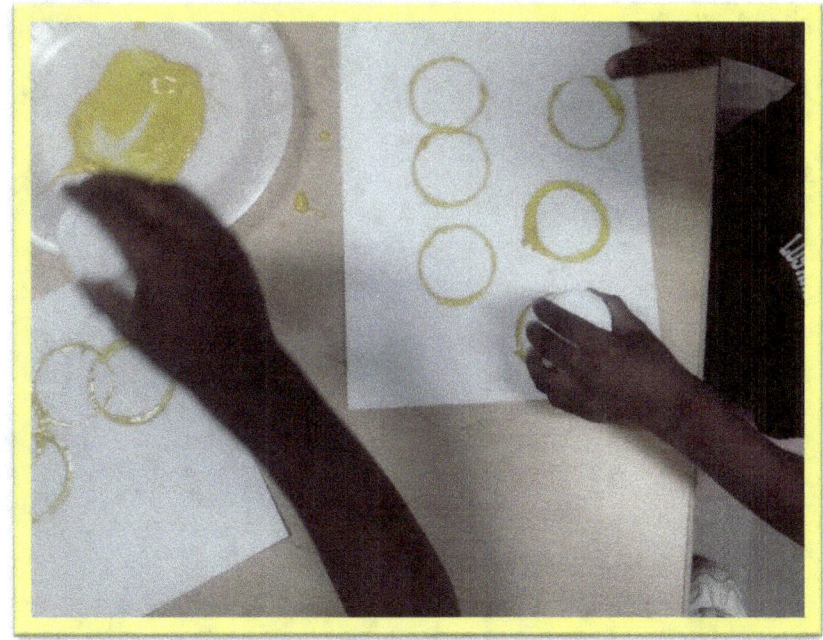

Instructions:

1. Lay out the sheet protector.
2. Lay out the sheet of paper.
3. Put a large enough drop of yellow paint on plate to be the width of the cup.
4. Dip the top of the cup into the yellow paint.
5. Then, place the cup on the paper to make circles. The circles can be in a row or overlap.

Making real-world connections with an
Accompanying activity, to reinforce learning and show children how art relates to their daily lives.

- *Activity:* Notice things in the environment that are yellow. The McDonald's arches are yellow. What else can you find that's yellow?

Unit #9: Printmaking

Activity #4 – Making circles with Primary colors

FOCUS:
Colors: red, blue, yellow
Shape: circle

MATERIALS:
surface protector
construction paper
paper plates
red paint
blue paint
yellow paint
styrofoam cups

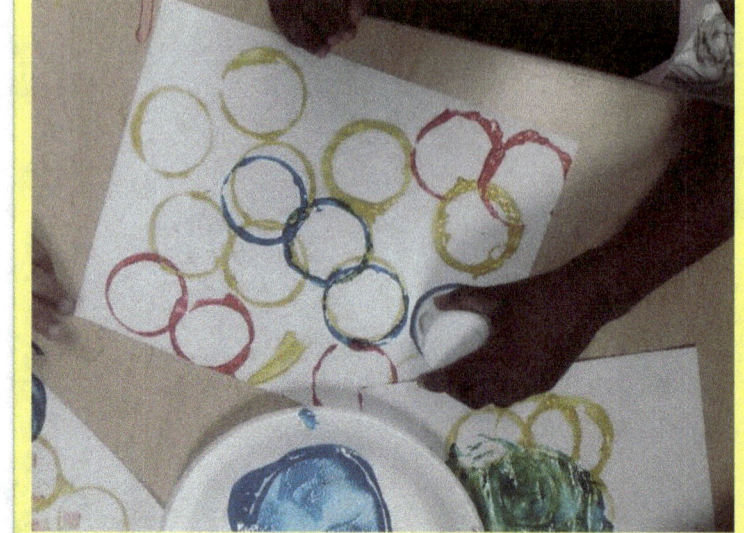

Instructions:

1. Lay out the surface protector.
2. Lay out the sheet of paper.
3. Put a large drop of red paint on a paper plate.
4. Put a large drop of blue paint on a paper plate.
5. Put a large drop of yellow paint on a paper plate.
6. Dip one cup into the red paint and make a circle on the paper.
7. Dip one cup into the blue paint and make a circle on the paper.
8. Dip one cup into the yellow paint and make a circle on the paper.
9. Repeat until you have the look you want.
    * This activity reinforces the Primary colors.

Making real-world connections with an
Accompanying activity, to reinforce learning and show children how art relates
to their daily lives.

- *Activity:* Notice things in the environment that are red. A stop sign is red. What else can you see that's red?

- *Activity:* Notice things in the environment that are blue. Maybe you can look for blue cars on a trip to the grocery store. Where else can you find something blue?

- *Activity*: Notice things in the environment that are yellow. The McDonald's arches are yellow. What else can you find that's yellow?

Unit #9: Printmaking

Activity# 5 - Making Lego prints with Primary colors

FOCUS: printmaking
red
blue
yellow
dots

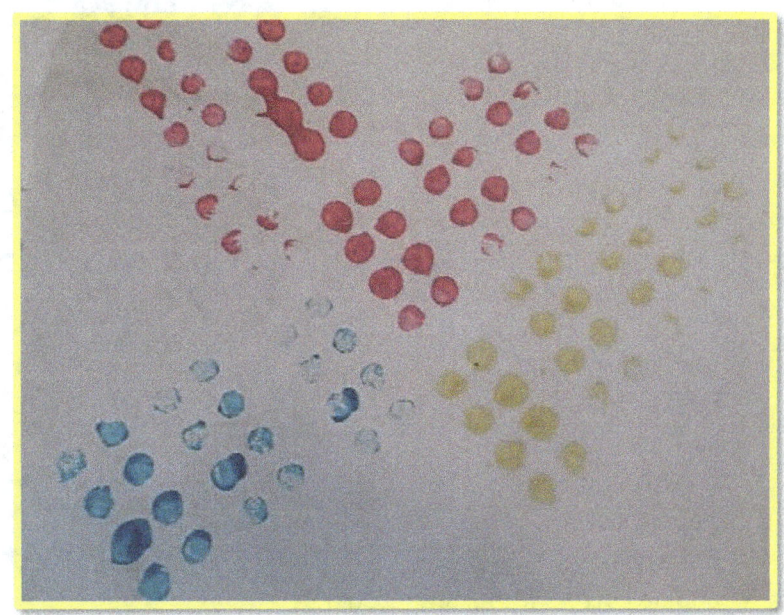

MATERIALS:
surface protector
construction paper
paper plates
red paint
blue paint
yellow paint
Legos

Instructions:

1. Lay out the surface protector.
2. Lay out the sheet of paper.
3. Put a large drop of red paint on a paper plate.
4. Put a large drop of blue paint on a paper plate.
5. Put a large drop of yellow paint on a paper plate.
6. Have your child use a separate Lego for each color of paint (dip circular side into paint).
7. Have your child dip one Lego into the red paint. Then, press the circular side of the Legos onto the paper to make Lego prints.
8. Have your child dip one Lego into the blue paint.
9. Then, press the circular side of the Lego onto the paper to make Lego prints.
10. Have your child dip one Lego into the yellow paint.
11. Then, press the circular side of the Lego onto the paper to make Lego prints.
*This activity can also be used to reinforce patterns by using one color and then the next in a sequence.

Making real-world connections with an
Accompanying activity, to reinforce learning and show children how art relates to their daily lives.

- *Activity:* **Build something with your Legos. As you are building, name the colors of the Legos you are using. Notice the small circles on the Legos.**

Unit #9: Printmaking

Activity #6 – Printmaking with the Secondary color green

FOCUS: Printmaking green

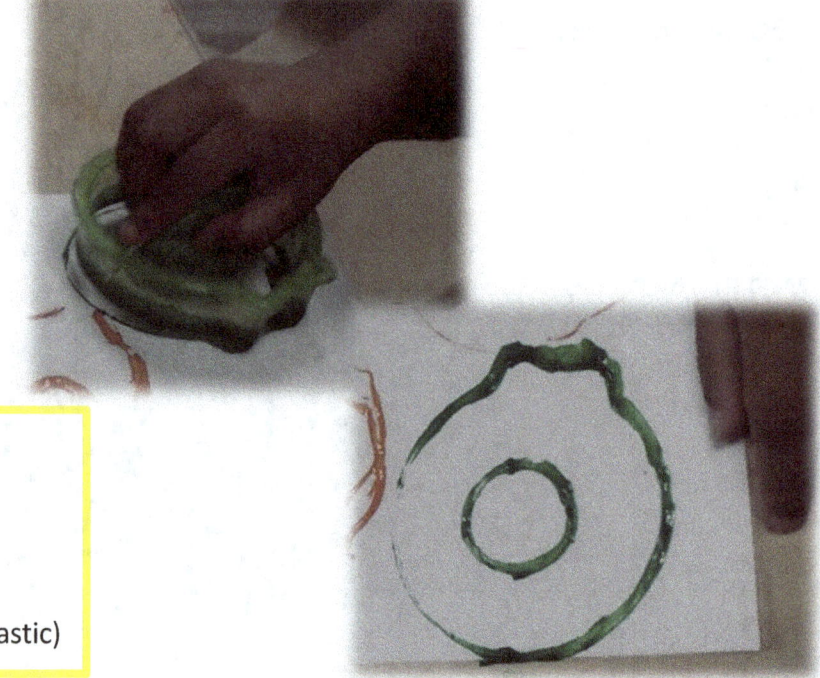

MATERIALS:
surface protector
construction paper
paper plates
green paint
cookie cutters (assorted plastic)

Instructions:

1. Lay out the surface protector.
2. Lay out the sheet of paper.
3. Put a large drop of green paint on a paper plate.
4. Have your child dip a cookie cutter into the green paint.
5. Then, have your child place the cookie cutter shape onto the paper to make prints.

*This is a fun project for any time of year. You can use holiday shapes around the holidays.

Making real-world connections with an
Accompanying activity, to reinforce learning and show children how art relates to their daily lives.

- *Activity:* **Look for things in the environment that are green. The leaves on the trees are green. The grass is green. What else can you find that's green?**

Unit #9: Printmaking

Activity# 7 - Printmaking using the Secondary color orange

FOCUS: Printmaking orange

MATERIALS:
surface protector
construction paper
paper plates
orange paint
cookie cutters

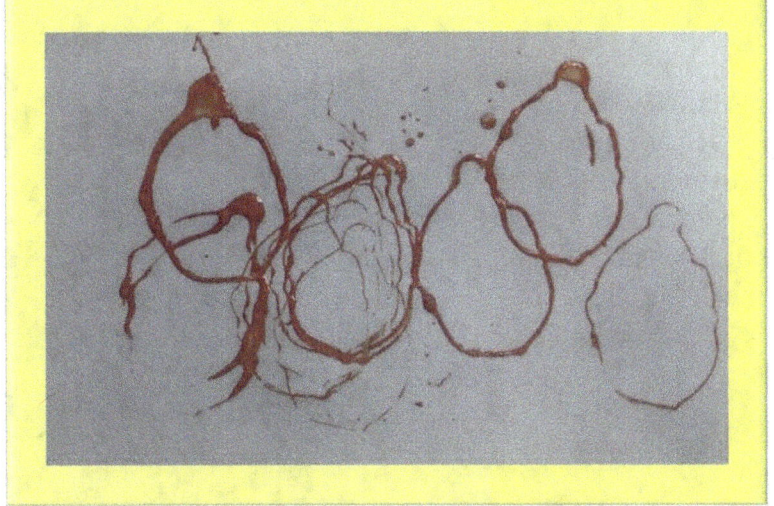

Instructions:

1. Lay out the surface protector.
2. Lay out the large paper.
3. Put a large drop of orange paint on a paper plate.
4. Have your child dip a cookie cutter into the orange paint.
5. Have your child place the cookie cutter on the paper to make prints.

*This is a fun project for any time of year. You can use holiday shapes around the holidays.

Making real-world connections with an
Accompanying activity, to reinforce learning and show children how art relates to their daily lives.

- *Activity:* **What can you find that is orange? Halloween is coming. Do you see Pumpkins and Jack-o-lanterns in the stores?**

Unit #9: Printmaking

Activity # 8 – Printmaking using the Secondary color purple

FOCUS: Printmaking
  purple

MATERIALS:
Surface protector
construction paper
paper plates
purple paint
cookie cutters

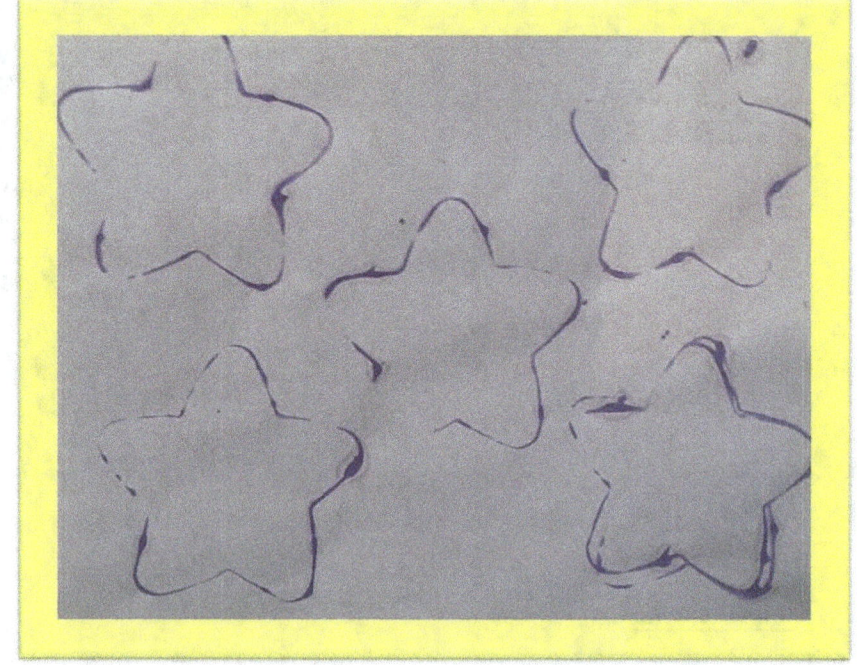

Instructions:

1. Lay out the surface protector.
2. Lay out the large white paper.
3. Put a large drop of purple paint on a paper plate.
4. Have your child dip a cookie cutter into the purple paint.
5. Have your child place the cookie cutter shape on the paper to make prints.

*This is a fun project for any time of year. You can use holiday shapes around the holidays.

Making real-world connections with an
Accompanying activity, to reinforce learning and show children how art relates to their daily lives.

• *Activity:* **What do you see that is purple? While you are shopping perhaps you can find some purple socks, or a purple ball.**

Unit #9: Printmaking

Activity #9-Secondary color prints (with cookie cutters)

FOCUS:
Printmaking
Secondary colors:
green
orange
purple

MATERIALS:
surface protector
construction paper
paper plates
green paint
orange paint
purple paint
cookie cutters

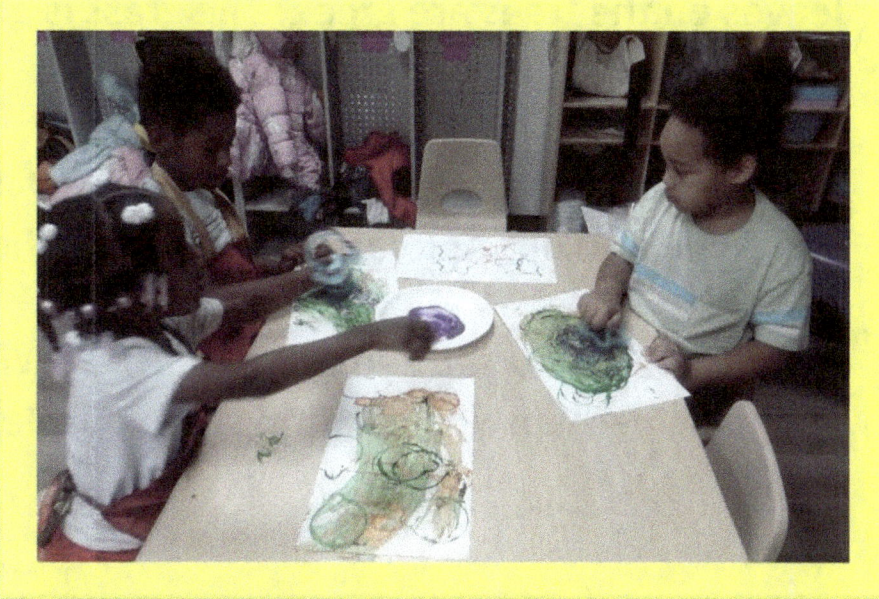

Instructions:

1. Lay out the surface protector.
2. Lay out the large paper.
3. Put a large drop of green paint on a paper plate.
4. Put a large drop of orange paint on a paper plate.
5. Put a large drop of purple paint on a paper plate.
6. Have your child use a separate cookie cutter for each color of paint.
7. Dip one cookie cutter into green.
8. Place the cookie cutter on the paper to make prints.
9. Dip one cookie cutter into orange.
10. Place the cookie cutter on the paper to make prints.
11. Dip one cookie cutter into purple.
12. Place the cookie cutter on the paper to make prints.
13. Repeat until you have a beautiful print work!

Making real-world connections with an
Accompanying activity, to reinforce learning and show children how art relates to their daily lives.

Accompanying activities are listed on the following page.

Activity: Look for things in the environment that are green. The leaves on the trees are green. The grass is green. What else can you find that's green?

Activity: What can you find that is orange? Around Halloween do you see Pumpkins and Jack-o-lanterns in the stores?

Activity: What do you see that is purple? While you are out shopping perhaps you can find some purple socks, or maybe a purple ball.

Unit #9: Printmaking

Activity #10 – Printmaking with the Secondary colors, using Legos

FOCUS: printmaking
Secondary colors:
green
orange
purple

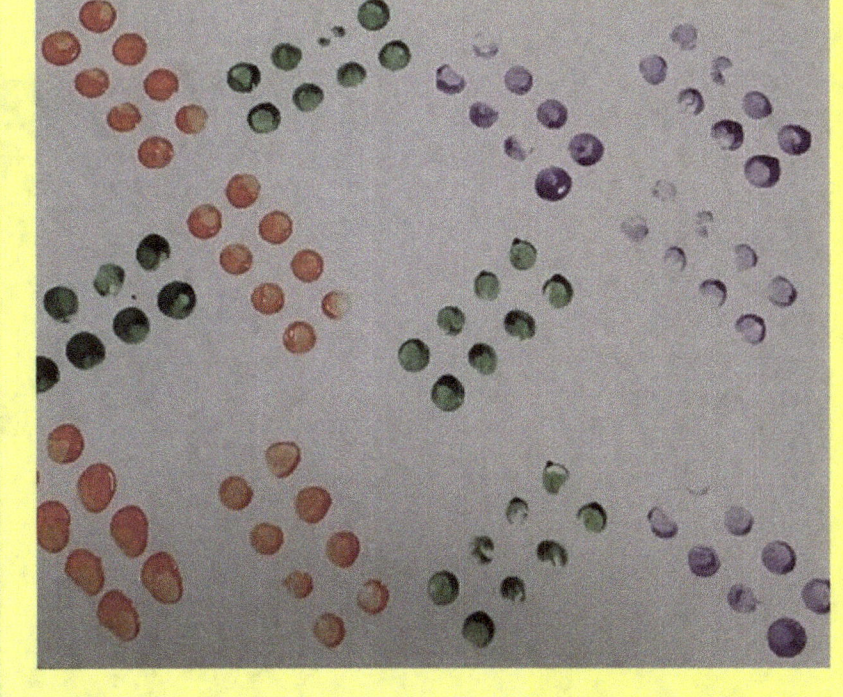

MATERIALS:
surface protector
construction paper
paper plates
green paint
orange paint
purple paint
Legos

Instructions:

1. Lay out the surface protector.
2. Lay out the construction paper.
3. Put a large drop of green paint on a paper plate.
4. Put a large drop of orange paint on a paper plate.
5. Put a large drop of purple paint on a paper plate.
6. Dip the side of the Lego with the circles into the paint.
7. Have your child dip one Lego into the green paint.
8. Place the Lego on the paper to make prints.
9. Have your child dip one Lego into orange.
10. Place the Lego on the paper to make prints.
11. Have your child dip one Lego into purple.
12. Place the Lego on the paper to make prints.

Making real-world connections with an
Accompanying activity, **to reinforce learning and show children how art relates**
to their daily lives.

- *Activity:* **Build something with your Legos. As you are building name the colors of the Legos you are using. Notice the small circles on the Legos.**

Unit #9: Printmaking

Activity #11 – Printmaking with fruit

FOCUS:
Printmaking
red

MATERIALS:
Surface protector
construction paper
paper plate
red paint
apple
knife
fork

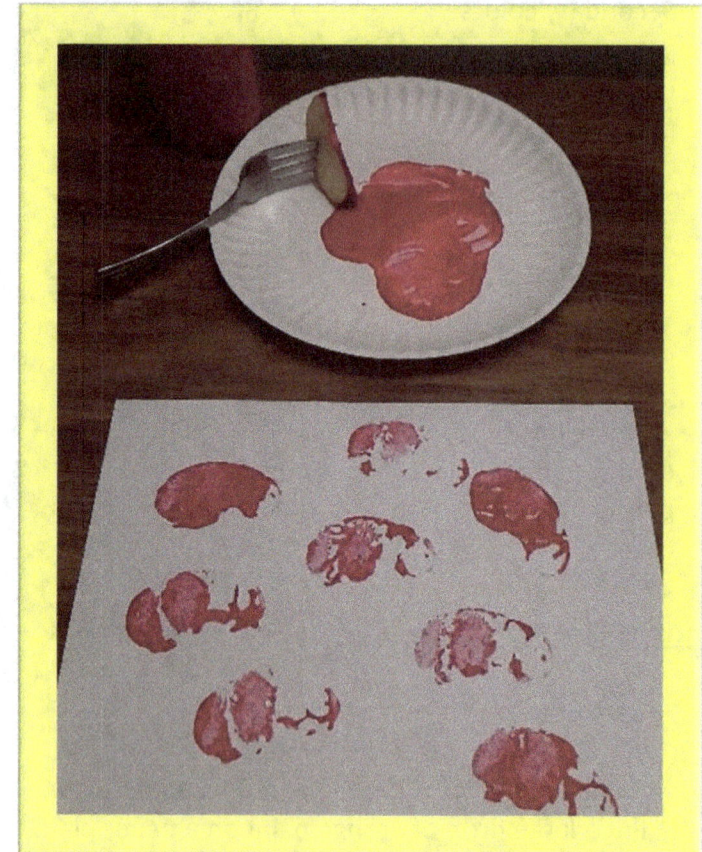

Instructions:

1. Lay out the surface protector.
2. Lay out the large paper.
3. Put a large drop of red paint on the paper plate.
4. Slice the apple in half. (Be sure your child is a safe distance from the knife to avoid getting cut.)
5. Stick the fork in the outside half of the apple and use it as a handle.
6. Have your child dip the apple into the red paint.
7. Have your child press the apple onto the paper to make apple prints.
   *(Be sure your child knows you cannot eat this apple.)

Making real-world connections with an
Accompanying activity, **to reinforce learning and show children how art relates to their daily lives.**

- *Activity:* **Go on a trip to the apple orchard. Pick some apples to take home to eat.**

Unit #9: Printmaking

Activity #12 – Printmaking with block prints

FOCUS:
Printmaking

MATERIALS:
surface protector
construction paper
leaf shaped print blocks
large orange, red and yellow ink pads

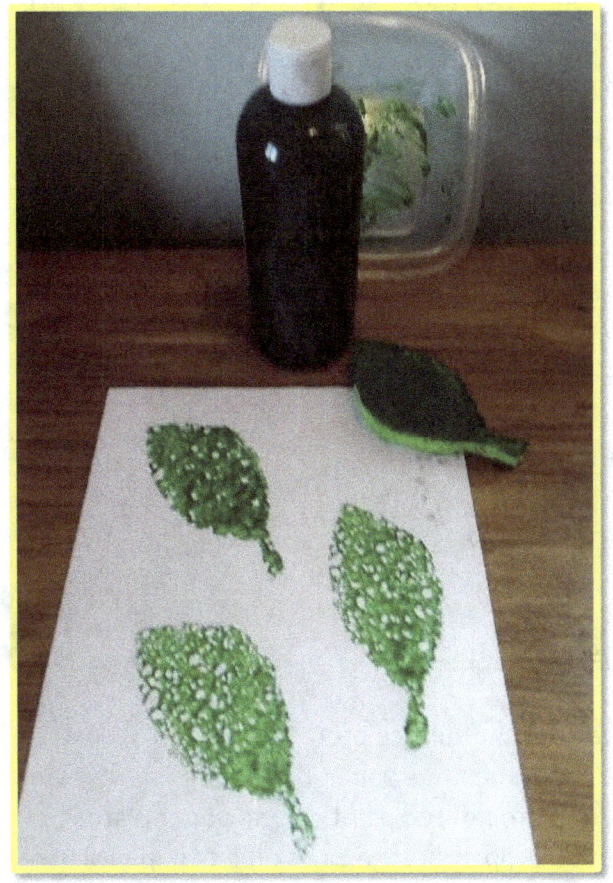

Instructions:

1. Lay out the surface protector.
2. Lay out the large paper.
3. Press a leaf block onto the ink pad.
4. Press the block onto the paper to make fall leaf prints.
5. Repeat.

**substitution: You can make a block print by cutting out a sponge in the shape of a leaf. Then, use either ink or paint to dip the sponge in.

Making real-world connections with an
Accompanying activity, **to reinforce learning and show children how art relates to their daily lives.**

- *Activity:* **Take a walk outside and notice the changing colors of the leaves.**

Unit #9: Printmaking

Activity #13 – Daytime Pumpkin patch

FOCUS:
Printmaking
red, yellow

MATERIALS:
surface protector
construction paper
red paint
orange paint
yellow paint
green crayon
2 potatoes
Knife
forks

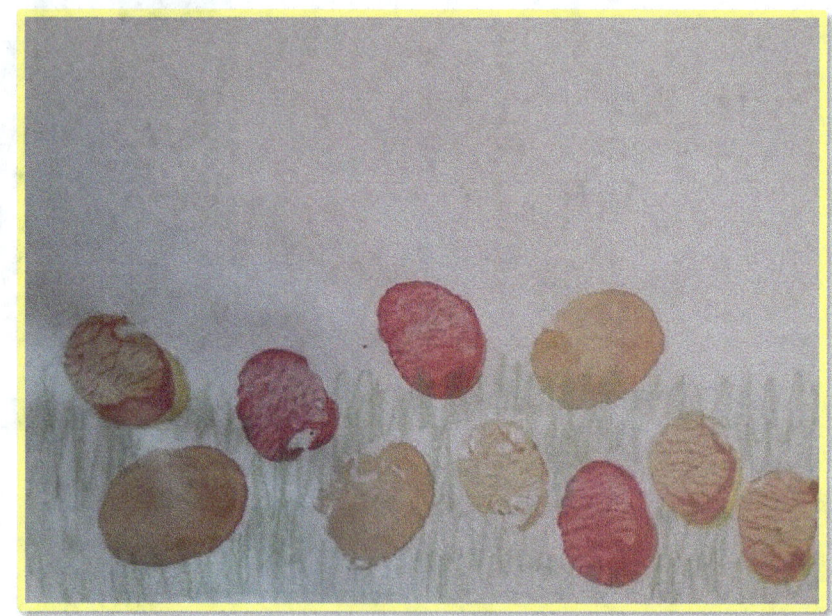

Instructions:

1 Lay out the surface protector.

2 Lay out the large paper.

3 Put a drop of red paint on one paper plate.

4 Put a drop of orange paint on one paper plate.

5 Put a drop of yellow paint on one paper plate.

6 Slice the potatoes in half. (Be sure your child is a safe distance from the knife).

7 Stick the forks into the outside of the potatoes to use as handles.

8 Have your child dip one potato slice into the red paint, one into the orange paint & one into the yellow paint.

9 Have your child dab the different colored potatoes onto the paper to make pumpkins.

10 Experiment using the red and yellow paint, adding some to the orange to create darker and lighter orange hues.

11 Have your child put as many pumpkins on the page as he/ she likes to make your pumpkin patch as big as your child likes it!

(*See the following page for* Mixing Hues)

Making real-world connections with an
Accompanying activity, **to reinforce learning and show children how art relates to their daily lives.**

- *Activity:* **Take a walk through the pumpkin patch. Notice the different colors of pumpkins.**

Mixing Hues

*How to mix a **lighter** orange hue:*
- Put some yellow on a paper plate.
- Slowly add a small amount of orange until you get the desired color.

*How to mix a **darker** orange hue:*
- Put some orange on a paper plate.
- Slowly add a small amount of red until you get the desired color.

Unit #9: Printmaking

Activity #14 – Nighttime pumpkin patch

FOCUS:
Printmaking
red
orange
yellow

MATERIALS:
surface protector
black construction paper
paper plate
red paint
orange paint
yellow paint
potatoes
knife
forks

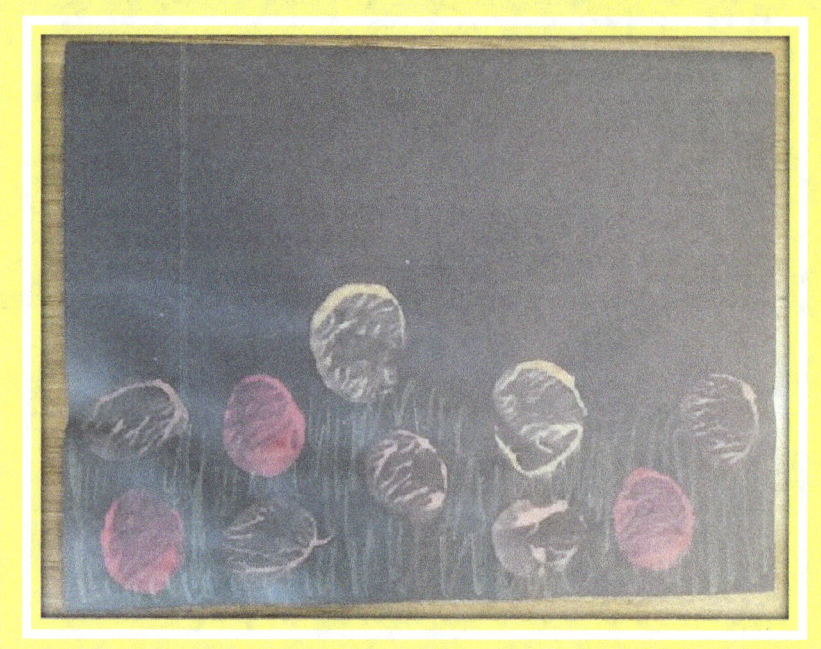

Instructions:

1. Lay out the surface protector.
2. Lay out the sheet of black paper.
3. Put drops of red, orange and yellow paints on separate paper plates.
4. Slice the potatoes in half. (Be sure your child is a safe distance from the knife to avoid getting cut).
5. Stick the forks into the outside of the potatoes to use as handles.
6. Place one potato slice into the red paint, one into the orange paint, and one into the yellow paint.
7. Have your child dab the different colored potatoes onto the paper to make pumpkins.
8. Experiment using the red and yellow paints, adding some to the orange to create darker and lighter orange hues.

(*See mixing hues instructions on the previous page.*)

Making real-world connections with an

Accompanying activity, to reinforce learning and show children how art relates to their daily lives.

- *Activity:* **Make your Pumpkin into a Jack-o-lantern and watch it light up at night.**

Unit ten: Collage
Introduction and explanation

The focus is on textures and creating interesting effects with collage. You will rip and cut paper and experiment with glue, feathers, and glitter! There will be several textures to feel.

Encourage your child to repeat the vocabulary words as you talk about each activity.

Vocabulary

Glue   flowers
Tissuepaper   glitter
Feathers

Learning styles addressed

Visual
Kinesthetic- fine motor, sensory

Learning connections

Art- texture

Sociology and History – Holidays: Thanksgiving, Christmas

Science – using flowers and leaves

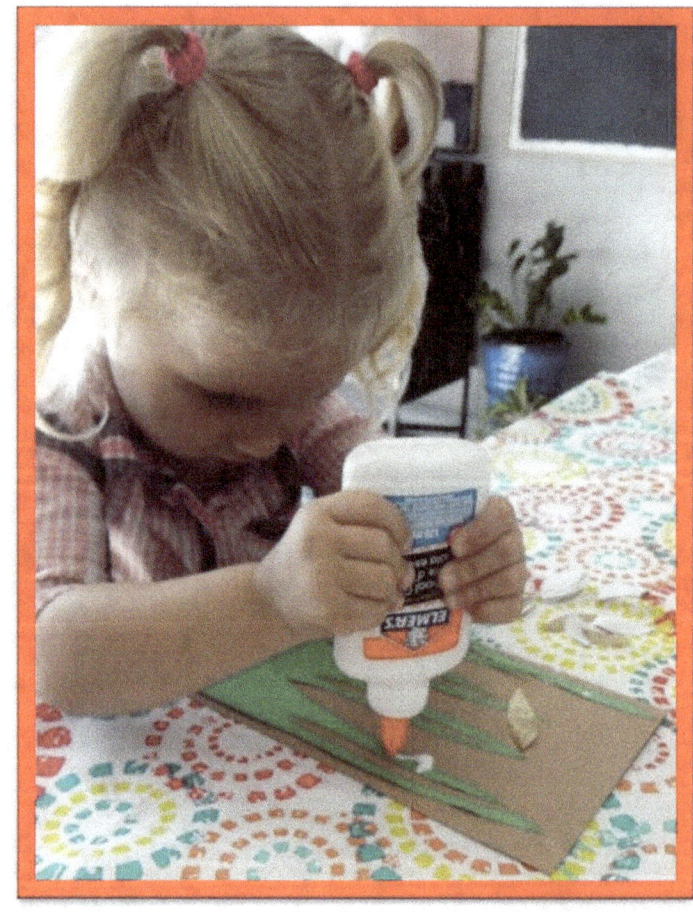

Unit #10: Collage

Activity #1 – Creating a tree from torn construction paper

FOCUS:
Collage
Manipulating materials by tearing

MATERIALS:
surface protector
black construction paper
red, orange, yellow &
brown construction paper
scissors
glue

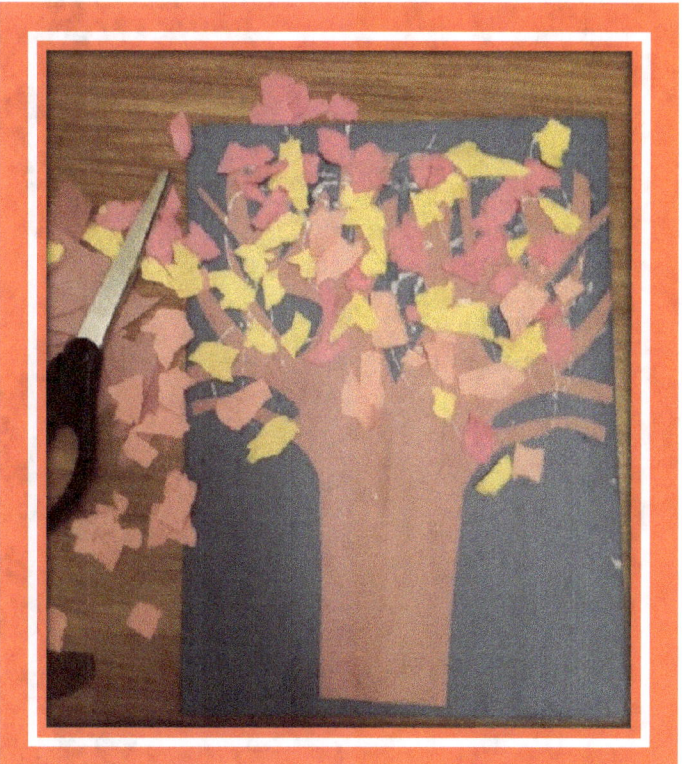

Instructions:

1. Lay out the surface protector.
2. Lay out the black paper.
3. Cut or tear a tree trunk from the brown construction paper.
4. Glue the trunk to the black paper.
5. Have your child tear and rip pieces of the red, orange and yellow construction paper to make fall leaves.
6. Put some glue on and around the top of the tree.
7. Have your child glue the red, orange, and yellow torn construction paper pieces to the top of the trunk to create a fall tree.

Making real-world connections with an
Accompanying activity, to reinforce learning and show children how art relates to their daily lives.

• **Reading: Book - Curious George Plants a tree.**

Unit #10: Collage

Activity #2 – Making a Jack-O-Lantern

FOCUS:
Collage
orange
black
triangle
Jack-O-Lantern

MATERIALS:
surface protector
black construction paper
paper plate
orange paint
scissors
glue stick

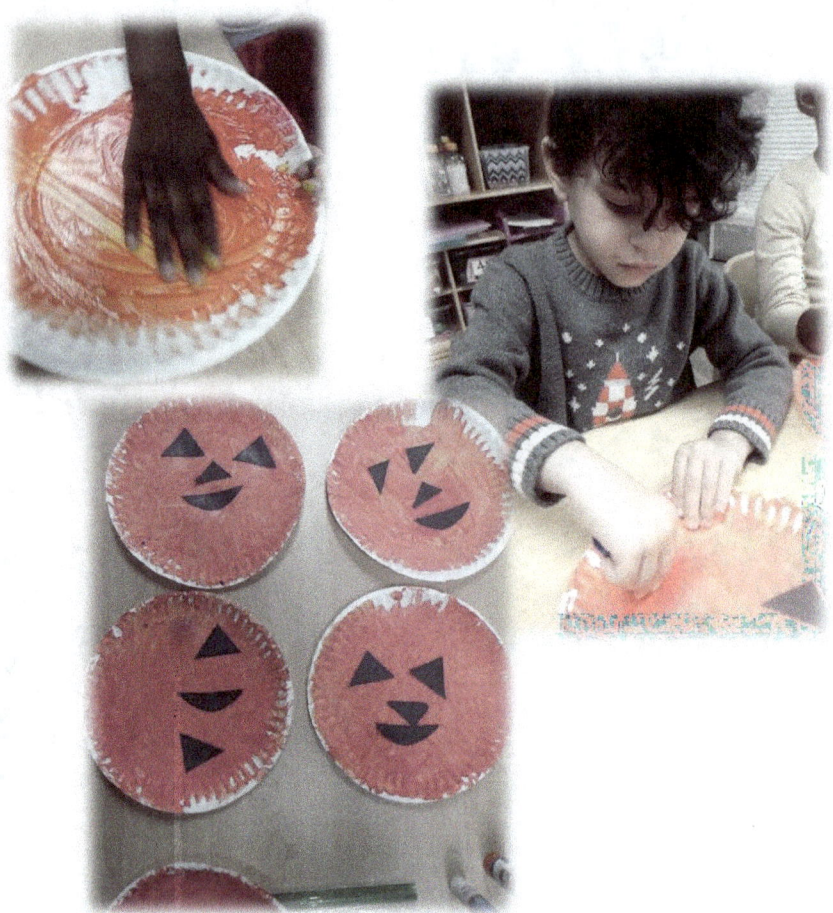

Instructions:

1. Lay out the surface protector.
2. Lay out the black construction paper.
3. Put a drop of orange paint on the paper plate.
4. Have your child spread the paint all over plate with his/ her fingers.
5. Cut out large and small triangles from the black construction paper.
6. Once the orange paint is dry, put some glue on the black triangles.
7. Have your child put the triangles on the plate to make a Jack-O-Lantern face.

Making real-world connections with an
Accompanying activity, to reinforce learning and show children how art relates to their daily lives.

- *Activity:* **Light up your Jack-o-Lantern by placing a battery-operated candle or light inside it.**

Unit #10: Collage

Activity #3 – Creating a fall wreath

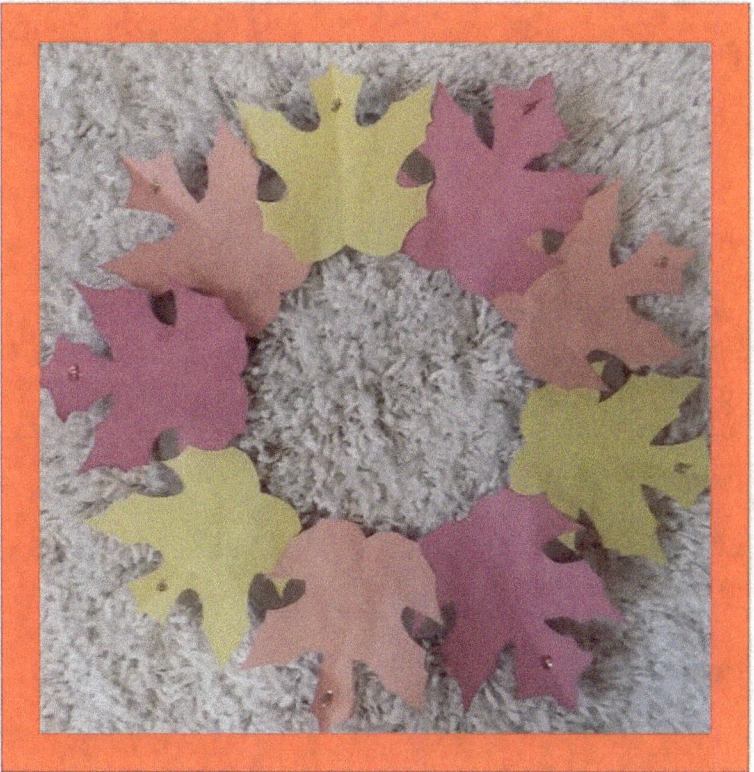

FOCUS:
Collage, Gluing

MATERIALS
surface protector
found, bought or
colored cut out leaves
brown paper bag
pencil
scissors
glue
glitter
plate for tracing
bowl for tracing

Instructions:

1. Lay out the surface protector.
2. Lay out the paper bag.
3. Draw a large circle on the brown paper bag by tracing the plate.
4. Draw a smaller circle inside the large circle by tracing the bowl.
5. Cut both circles out.
6. If making leaves from construction paper, cut out your leaves.
7. Put some glue on the paper bag circle.
8. Have your child put the leaves on the cut-out wreath made from the paper bag.
9. Glue the leaves in place.

**Optional: Put drops of glue on the leaves and sprinkle glitter on top to make your decorative fall wreath.

Making real-world connections with an
Accompanying activity, to reinforce learning and show children how art relates to their daily lives.

- **Activity: Go for a nature walk ahead of time to collect colorful leaves.**

Unit #10: Collage

Activity #4 – Dried flower collage

FOCUS:
Collage

MATERIALS:
Surface protector
white, tan or beige construction paper
dried flower petals from garden or nature walk
mums, marigolds, roses, dried leaves
or cut out flower petals from construction paper
paint brush
glue
water

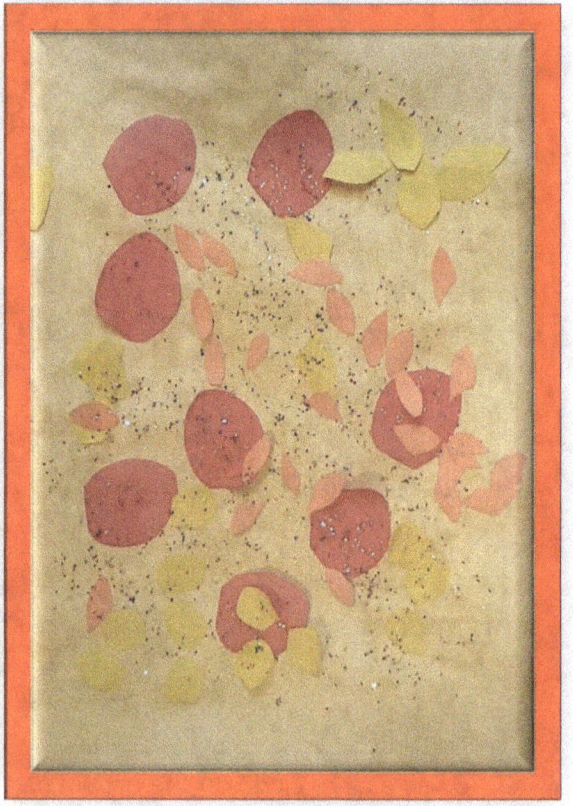

Instructions:

1. Lay out the surface protector.
2. Lay out the sheet of paper.
3. Pull apart the dried flowers.
4. Mix glue and water - 1-part glue to 1-part water.
5. Help your child spread the glue mixture on the paper with the paintbrush.
6. Have your child sprinkle the dried flowers onto the paper to create a dried flower collage.
7. If desired, add a little glitter.

Making real-world connections with an
Accompanying activity, to reinforce learning and show children how art relates to their daily lives.

- *Activity:* **Go for a nature walk ahead of time to collect colorful leaves.**

Unit #10: Collage

Activity #5 – collage

FOCUS:
Collage
Gluing feathers

MATERIALS:
surface protector
white construction paper
brown construction paper
pencil
scissors
glue
small googly eyes
assorted feathers

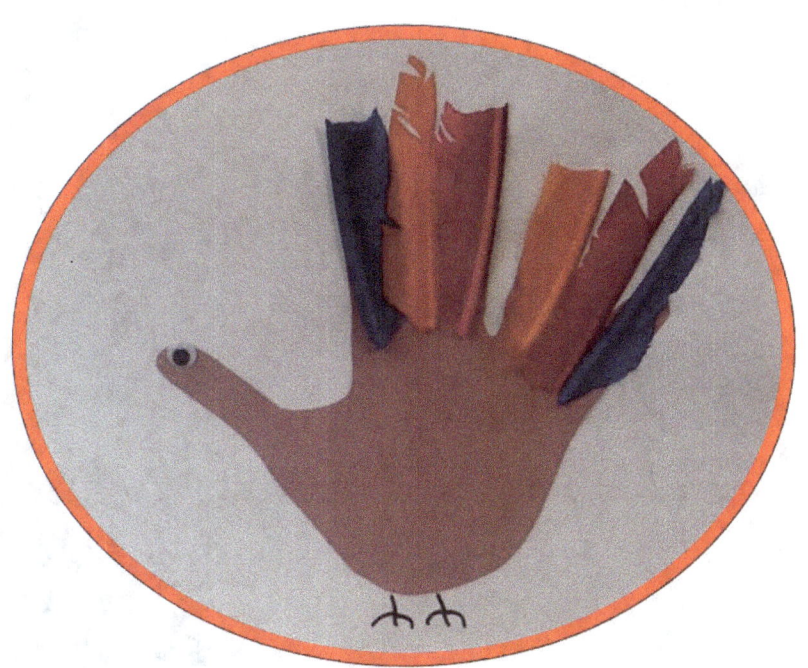

Instructions:

1. Lay out the surface protector.
2. Lay out the white paper.
3. Place your child's hand on the brown construction paper and trace around it with the pencil.
4. Cut out your child's turkey shaped handprint.
5. Help your child glue the turkey handprint to the white paper.
6. Help your child put some glue on the turkey.
7. Have your child decorate the turkey by gluing on feathers to make tail feathers.
8. Put a googly eye on the thumbprint so your Turkey can see!

Making real-world connections with an
Accompanying activity, to reinforce learning and show children how art relates to their daily lives.

- *Read:* **Twas the day after Thanksgiving: a lift-the-flap story.**

Unit #10: Collage

Activity #6 – Collage headband

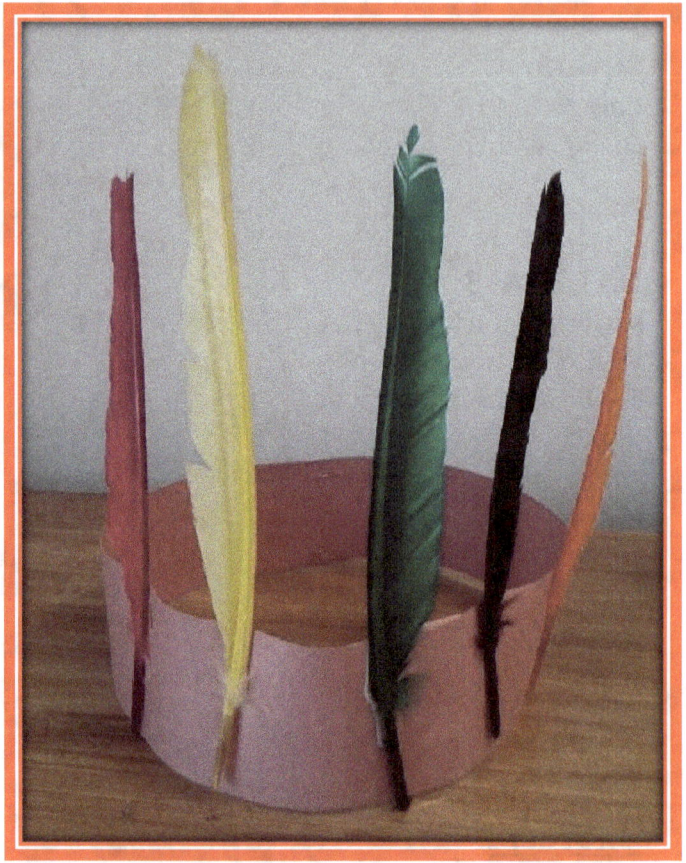

FOCUS:
collage
gluing feathers

MATERIALS:
surface protector
brown construction paper
assorted feathers
scissors
glue
tape
tape measure (optional)

Instructions:

1. Lay out the surface protector.
2. Decide on the length of the headband by measuring your child's head.
3. Cut out the desired length from two pieces of construction paper.
4. Tape the pieces of construction paper together.
5. Wrap the headband around your child's head and measure it to fit.
6. Lay the headband on a flat surface.
7. Have your child glue feathers to the headband to decorate it.
8. Once dry, tape the headband to fit snuggly around your child's head.

Making real-world connections with an
Accompanying activity, to reinforce learning and show children how art relates to their daily lives.

- *Website:* Google "Native American Headdress" and look at picturesof Native American Headdresses.

Unit #10: Collage

Activity #7 – Creating a Thanksgiving feast

FOCUS:
Collage
Gluing magazines

MATERIALS:
surface protector
paper plate
magazines with pictures of food or
printed pictures of food
child-safe scissors
glue stick

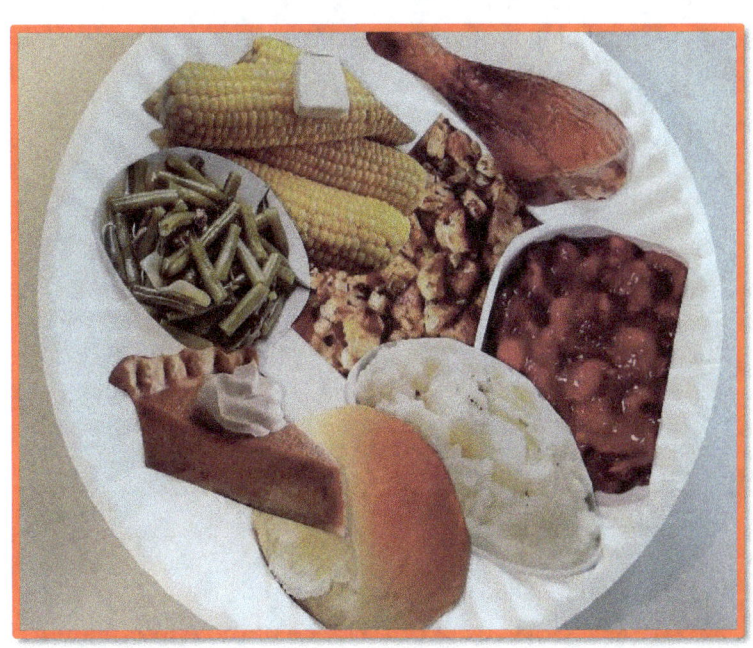

Instructions:

1. Lay out the surface protector.
2. Help your child cut out pictures of food to represent a Thanksgiving feast.
3. Have your child put the pictures of food wherever they like on the paper plate.
4. Help your child glue the pictures on the paper plate to represent your family's Thanksgiving feast.

Making real-world connections with an
Accompanying activity, to reinforce learning and show children how art relates to their daily lives.

- *Read:* **The first Thanksgiving: A lift-flap book.**

Unit #10: Collage

Activity #8– Corn on the cob

FOCUS:
Collage
Gluing tissue paper

MATERIALS:
surface protector
green construction paper
green tissue paper
small pieces of yellow tissue paper
paper plate
scissors
glue

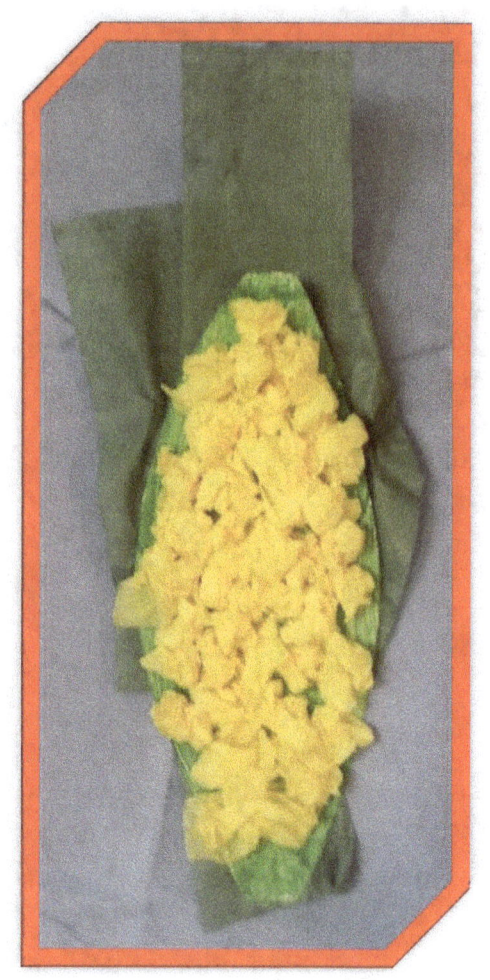

Instructions:

1. Lay out the surface protector.
2. Use scissors to cut out a piece of the paper plate to form the shape of an ear of corn.
3. Show your child how to crumble tissue paper into small balls.
4. Pour glue all over the cut-out paper plate, ear of corn shape.
5. Help your child glue the tissue paper balls onto the ear of corn.
6. Cut strips of the green construction paper.
7. Glue some green tissue paper to the top of the corn to look like husks.

Making real-world connections with an
Accompanying activity, to reinforce learning and show children how art relates to their daily lives.

- *Youtube video:* Watch Why does popcorn pop? Science for kids. You Tube. Make popcorn and eat it!

Unit #10: Collage

Activity #9 – Pumpkin pie

FOCUS:
Collage
Gluing paper

MATERIALS:
surface protector
paper plate
orange construction paper
brown construction paper
glue
cotton balls
scissors

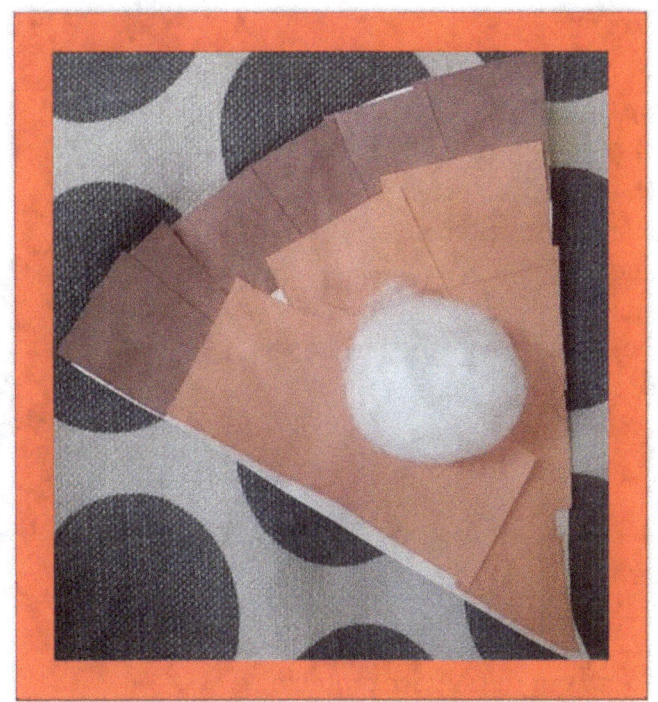

Instructions:

1. Lay out the surface protector.
2. Cut out a pie piece shape from the paper plate.
3. Cut out small squares from the brown construction paper.
4. Cut out small squares from the orange construction paper.
5. Put some liquid glue on the pie piece.
6. Help your child glue the brown squares to the curved edge of the pie piece to make the crust.
7. Help your child glue the orange construction paper squares to the paper plate for the pie filling.
8. Help your child glue a cotton ball on top of the orange construction paper squares for the whipped topping!

Making real-world connections with an
Accompanying activity, to reinforce learning and show children how art relates to their daily lives.
• *Activity:* **Treat your tummy and eat a slice of Pumpkin pie.**

Unit #10: Collage

Activity #10– Catching a fish for planting

> **FOCUS:**
> Collage
> Gluing

> **MATERIALS:**
> Surface protector
> white construction paper
> blue construction paper
> blue marker
> liquid glue
> sheet of gray construction paper
> *(or color of choice)*

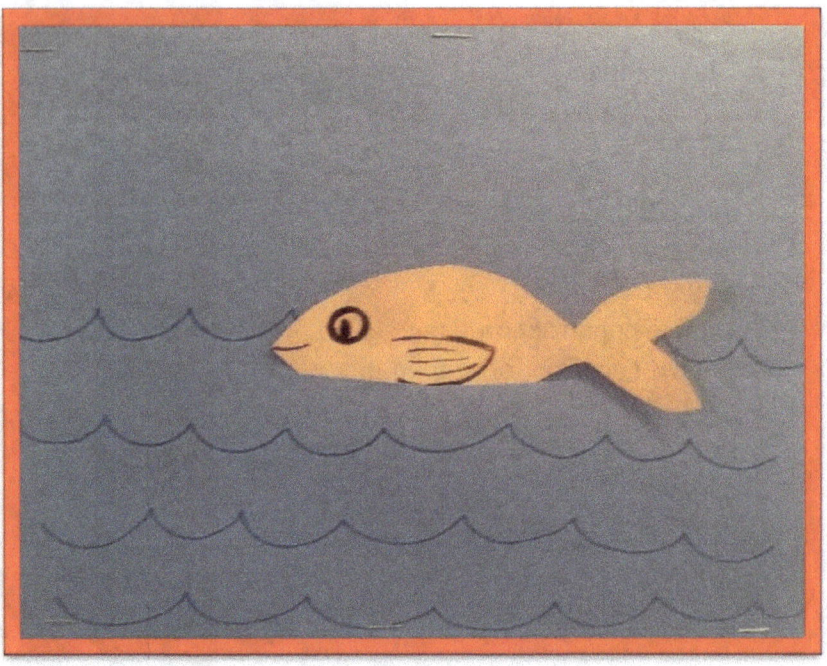

Instructions:

1. Lay out the surface protector.
2. Use the scissors to cut a lengthwise horizontal slit in the center of the blue paper.
3. Staple the edges of the blue and white construction paper together, all the way around.
4. Use the fish template to cut out your fish from the gray (or preferred color construction paper).
5. Help your child draw an eye, a mouth and a fin on the side of the fish.
6. Have your child use the blue marker to draw waves on the blue construction paper.
7. Put the fish's head in the water with his tail sticking up. (slide it into the slit)
8. Your child can make the fish go in and out of the water.
9. Can you catch a fish to plant with your corn?

Making real-world connections with an
Accompanying activity, to reinforce learning and show children how art relates to their daily lives.

- *Read:* **Squanto and the First Thanksgiving. This book tells about Squanto and how he taught the pilgrims to grow corn by planting the seeds with a fish.**

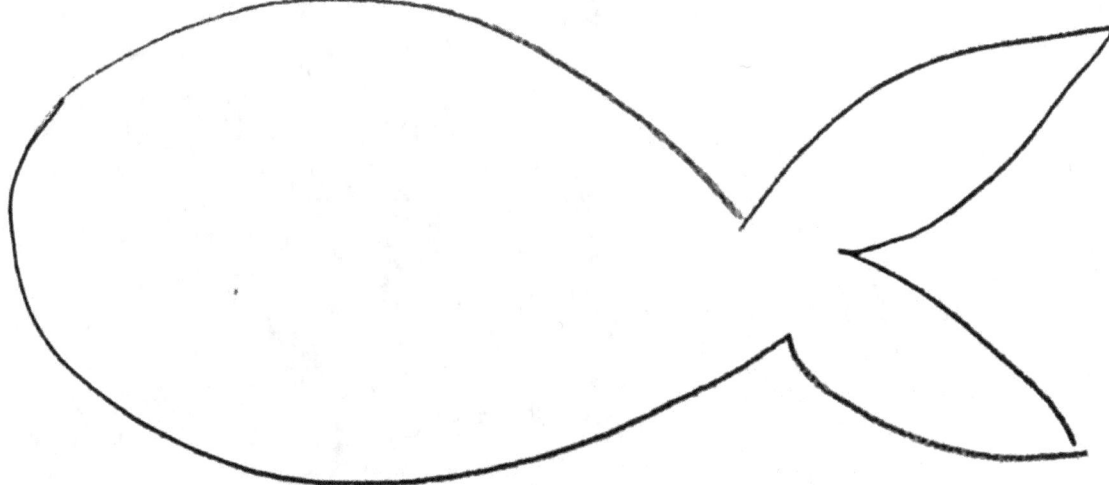

Unit #10: Collage

Activity #11– Decorating a Christmas tree

FOCUS:
Collage
gluing construction paper

MATERIALS:
surface protector
green and red construction paper
hole punch
pencil
scissors
glue
glitter
Christmas tree template

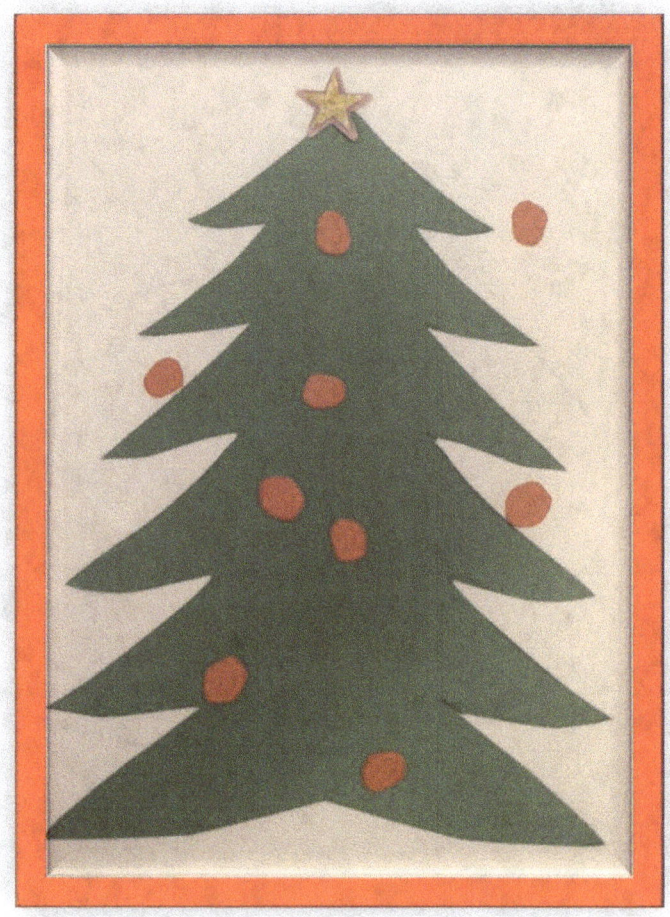

Instructions:

1. Lay out the surface protector.
2. With the pencil, trace the Christmas tree template onto the green construction paper.
3. Cut out the green Christmas tree.
4. With the hole punch, punch out circles from the red construction paper.
5. Put small drops of glue all over the green Christmas tree.
6. Help your child glue the red circles on the Christmas tree for ornaments.
   *Optional: Sprinkle glitter on the Christmas tree for added sparkle.

Making real-world connections with an
Accompanying activity, to reinforce learning and show children how art relates to their daily lives.

- *Read:* **Touch and Feel Christmas.**

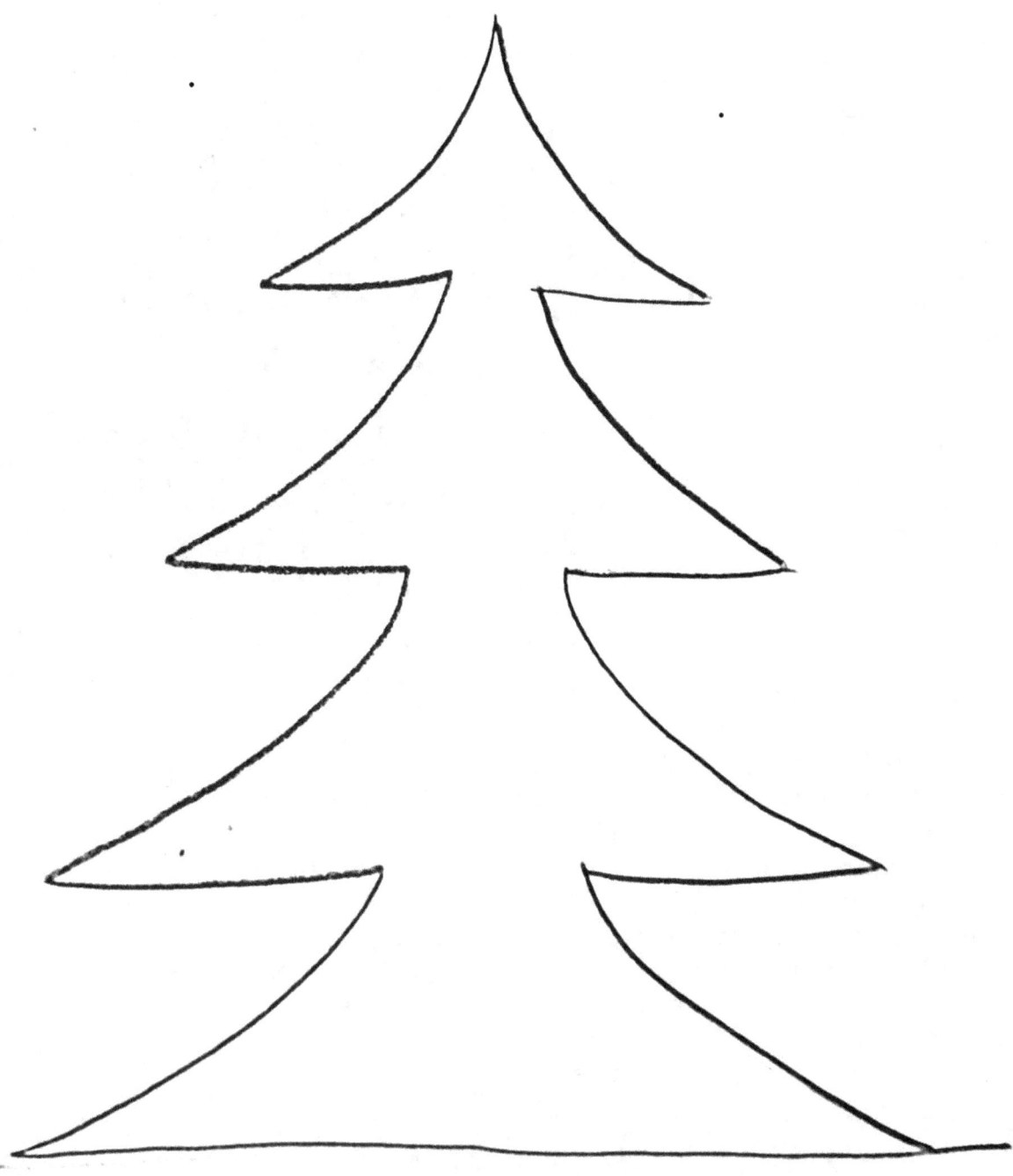

Unit #10: Collage

Activity #12- Mistletoes

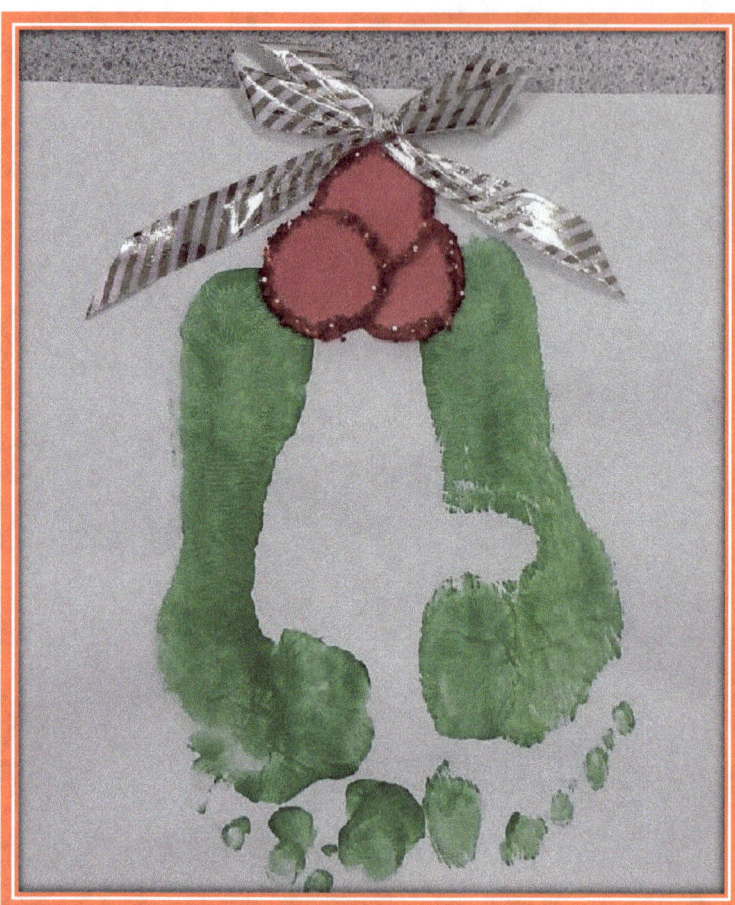

FOCUS:
Collage

MATERIALS:
Surface protector
white construction paper
red construction paper
green paint
paintbrush
pencil
scissors
glue
red glitter
silver or gold ribbon
hole punch
baby wipes

Instructions:

1. Lay out the surface protector.
2. Lay out the white paper.
3. Paint the bottom of your child's feet with green paint.
4. Have your child step lightly onto the white paper, leaving footprints.
5. Wipe your child's feet off with the wipes.
6. When the paint is dry, cut out a few small (quarter sized) red circles from the construction paper for berries.
7. Help your child glue the berries to the tops of the heels.
8. Cut out the Mistletoes.
9. Use the hole punch to make a hole at the top of the berries.
10. String the ribbon through the hole and tie a bow.
11. You are ready to hang your mistletoes!

Making real-world connections with an
Accompanying activity, **to reinforce learning and show children how art relates to their daily lives.**

- *Activity:* **Give your child a kiss under the Mistletoe.**

Unit #10: Collage

Activity #13 – Gingerbread man

FOCUS:
Collage
Gluing

MATERIALS:
surface protector
brown construction paper
black construction paper
pencil
scissors
glue
hole punch
Gingerbread man pattern
(included)

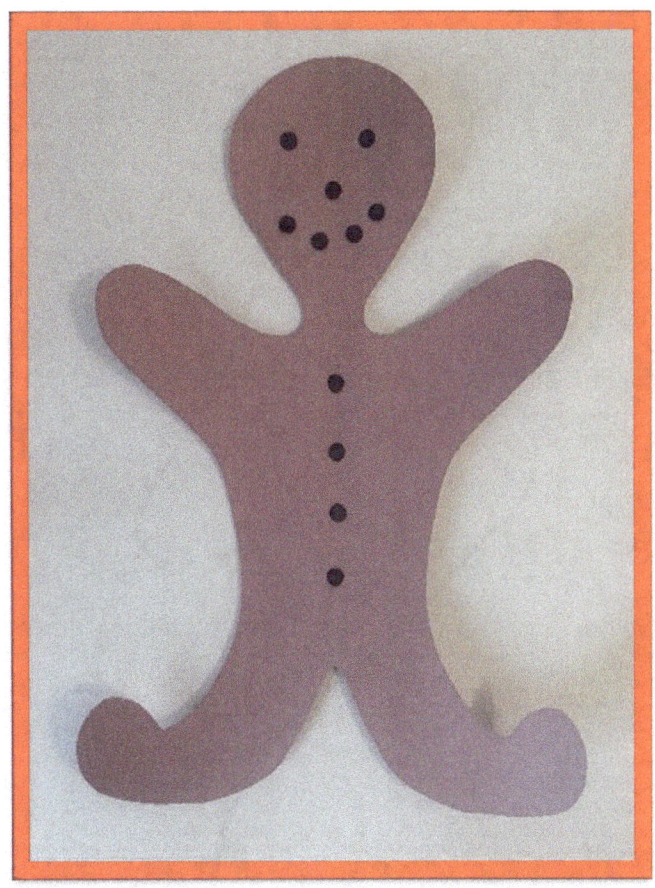

Instructions:

1. Draw a gingerbread man on the brown construction paper by tracing the enclosed pattern.
2. Cut out the gingerbread man with the scissors.
3. Punch out eleven black circles using the hole punch for the eyes, nose, mouth and buttons.
4. Help your child glue on the black circles in the appropriate places.
5. Glue on two black circles for the eyes.
6. Glue on one black circle for the nose.
7. Glue on six black circles for the mouth.
8. Glue on several black circles for buttons on the chest of the gingerbread man.

Making real-world connections *with an*

Accompanying activity, **to reinforce learning and show children how art relates to their daily lives.**

- ***Activity:* Bake Gingerbread cookies and eat them.**

Gingerbread Template

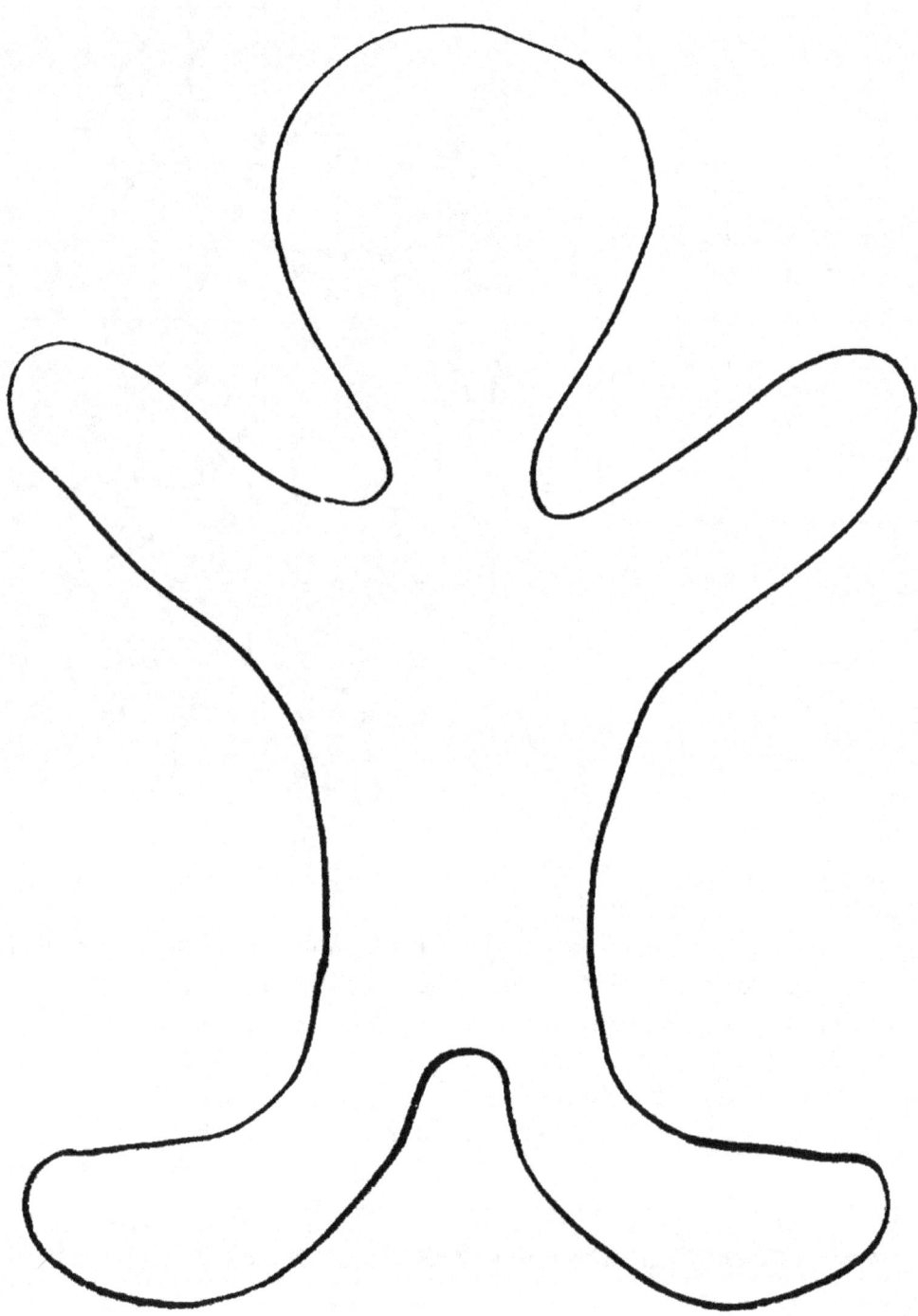

Unit #10: Collage

Activity #14 – Christmas ornament

FOCUS:
Collage
Gluing glitter

MATERIALS:
Surface protector
poster board
pencil
scissors
glue
paint brush
assorted markers
glitter
hole punch
ribbon
Christmas ornament template

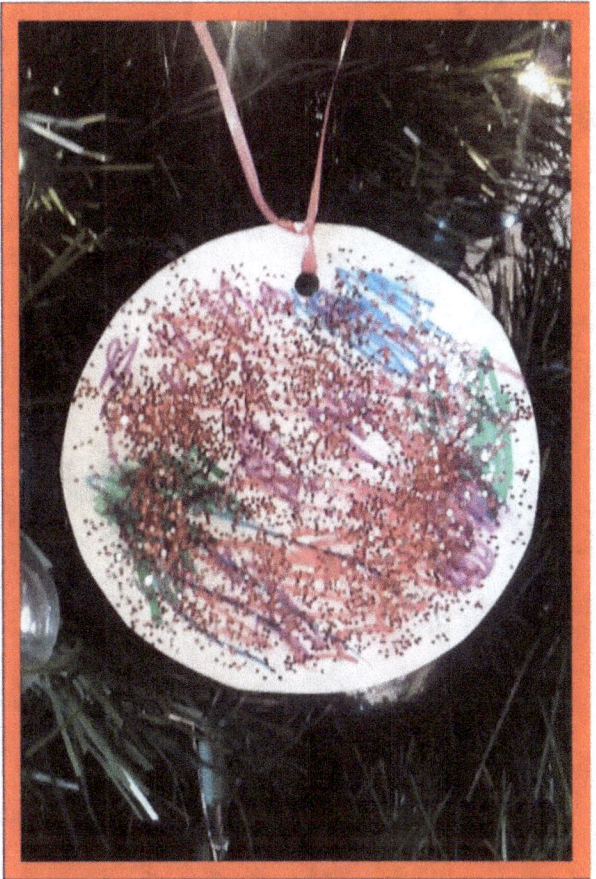

Instructions:

1. Lay out the surface protector.
2. Use the pencil to trace the Christmas ornament template onto the poster board.
3. Cut out the ornament.
4. Use the hole punch to punch out a circle at the top of the ornament.
5. Have your child color both sides of the ornament with markers, making an original design.
6. Allow a few minutes for the markers to dry.
7. Put some glue on the paintbrush and help your child spread it over the ornament.
8. Help your child sprinkle glitter on the ornament.
9. When the glitter is dry, string the ribbon through the hole and tie it, leaving enough room to hang the ornament on the Christmas tree.

Making real-world connections with an

Accompanying activity, **to reinforce learning and show children how art relates to their daily lives.**

• *Activity:* **Hang your ornament on the Christmas tree.**

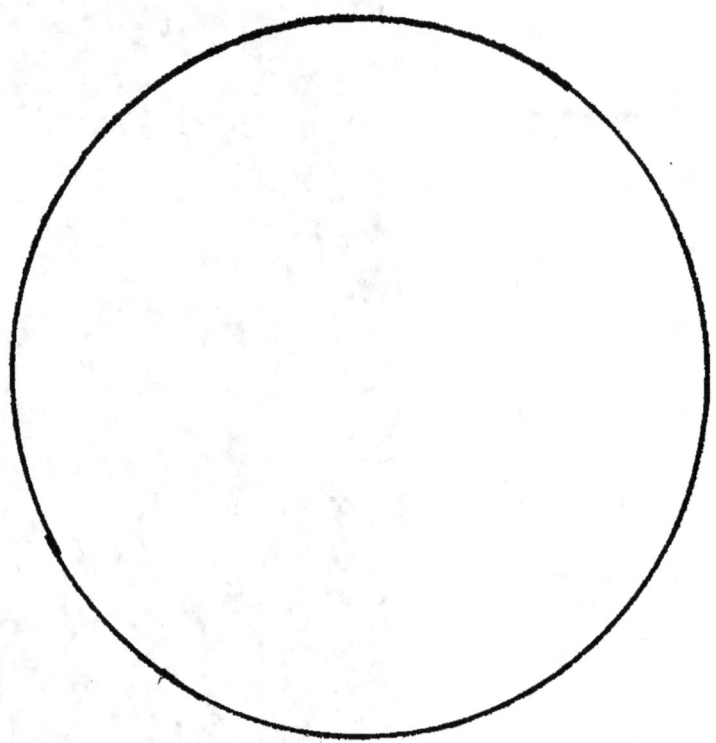

Unit #10: Collage

Activity #15 – Christmas tree star

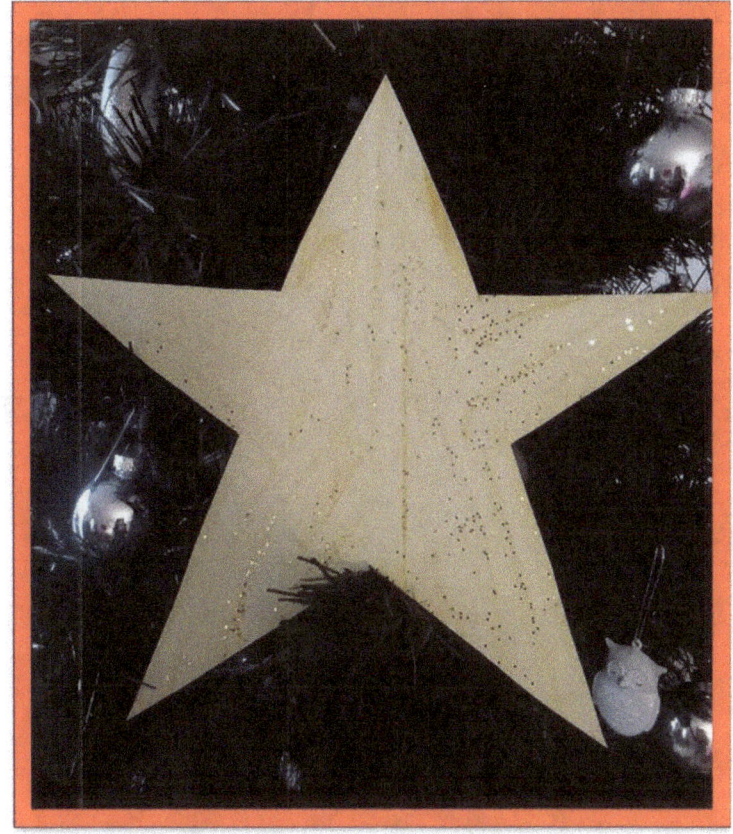

MATERIALS:
Surface protector
poster board
pencil
yellow paint
paintbrush
scissors
glue
cable tie
gold glitter

Instructions:

1. Lay out the surface protector.
2. Using the pencil and the star template, trace the star onto the poster board.
3. Use scissors to cut out the star.
4. Place some yellow paint on the paper plate.
5. Have your child paint the star with yellow paint.
6. While the paint is still wet, help your child sprinkle the gold glitter onto the star.
7. Once the star is dry, attach the middle part of the cable tie to the back of the star with glue.
8. Let the star dry overnight.
9. Use the cable tie to attach the star to the Christmas tree by wrapping it around a top branch.
10. Your child's artwork is featured atop your tree!

Making real-world connections with an
Accompanying activity, to reinforce learning and show children how art relates to their daily lives.

- *Activity:* **Put the star on your Christmas tree.**

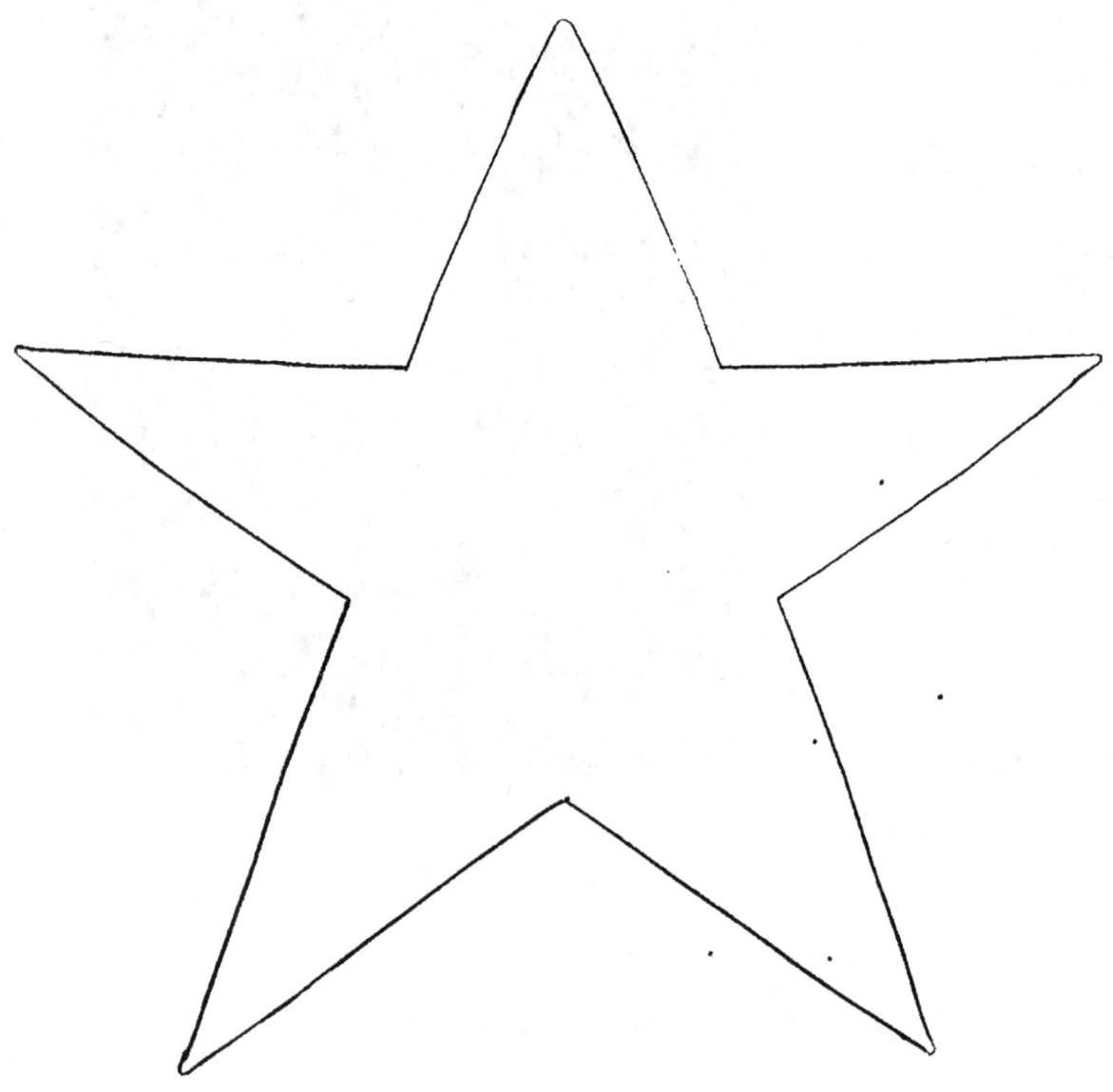

Unit #10: Collage

Activity #16 – Blizzard scene

FOCUS:
Gluing cotton
Gluing glitter

MATERIALS:
Surface protector
blue construction paper
glue
cotton balls
fine silver glitter (*optional)

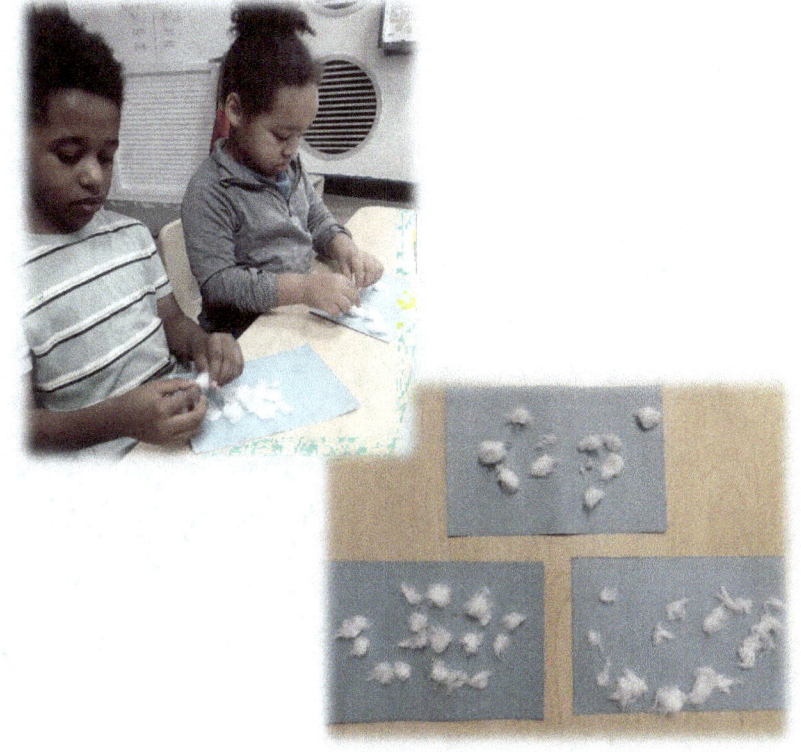

Instructions:

1. Lay out the surface protector.
2. Lay out the blue construction paper.
3. Show your child how to drop glue on the paper by turning the glue bottle upside down and squeezing.
4. Have your child drop dots of glue all over the blue construction paper.
5. Help your child pull the cotton balls apart to make smaller balls or pieces.
6. Have your child glue the cotton pieces to the construction paper.
7. Help your child sprinkle glitter all over the cotton to make a sparkly blizzard scene.

Making real-world connections with an
Accompanying activity, to reinforce learning and show children how art relates to their daily lives.

- *Read:* **The Snowy Day by Ezra Jack Keats**

Unit #10: Collage

Activity #17 – Night time Blizzard

FOCUS:
Gluing cotton
Gluing glitter

MATERIALS:
surface protector
black construction paper
glue
cotton balls
fine silver glitter (*optional)

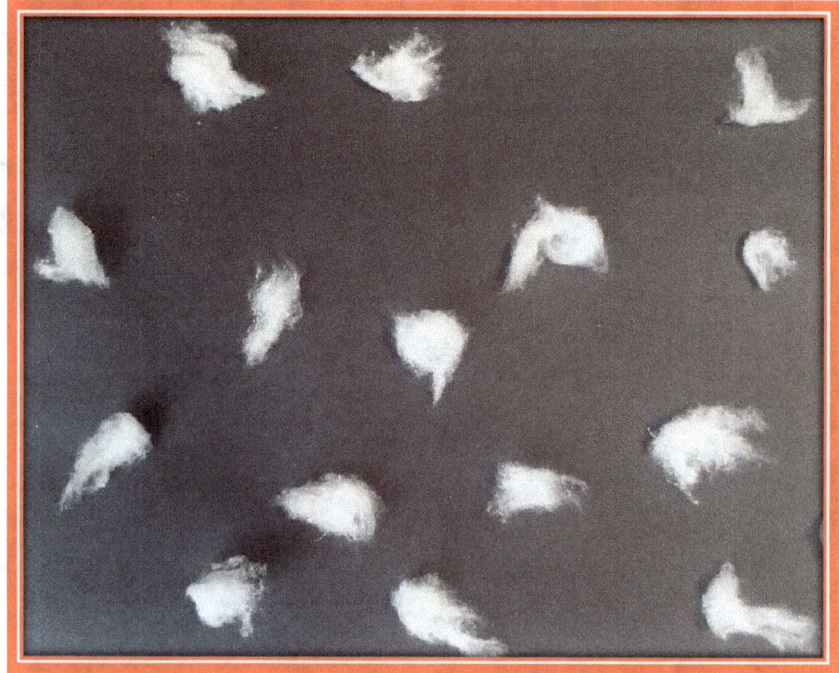

Instructions:

1. Lay out the surface protector.
2. Lay out the black construction paper.
3. Remind your child of how you placed dots of glue on the blue paper. (previous project)
4. Have your child place dots of glue all over the black construction paper.
5. Help your child pull the cotton balls apart to make smaller balls or pieces.
6. Have your child glue the cotton pieces onto the construction paper.
7. Help your child sprinkle glitter all over the cotton to make a sparkling nighttime blizzard scene. (*optional)

Making real-world connections with an
Accompanying activity, to reinforce learning and show children how art relates to their daily lives.
- *Activity:* **Watch it snow.**

Unit #10: Collage

Activity #18 – Making a Snowman

FOCUS:
Gluing marshmallows
Gluing glitter

MATERIALS:
Surface protector
blue construction paper
glue
large marshmallows
silver glitter (*optional)

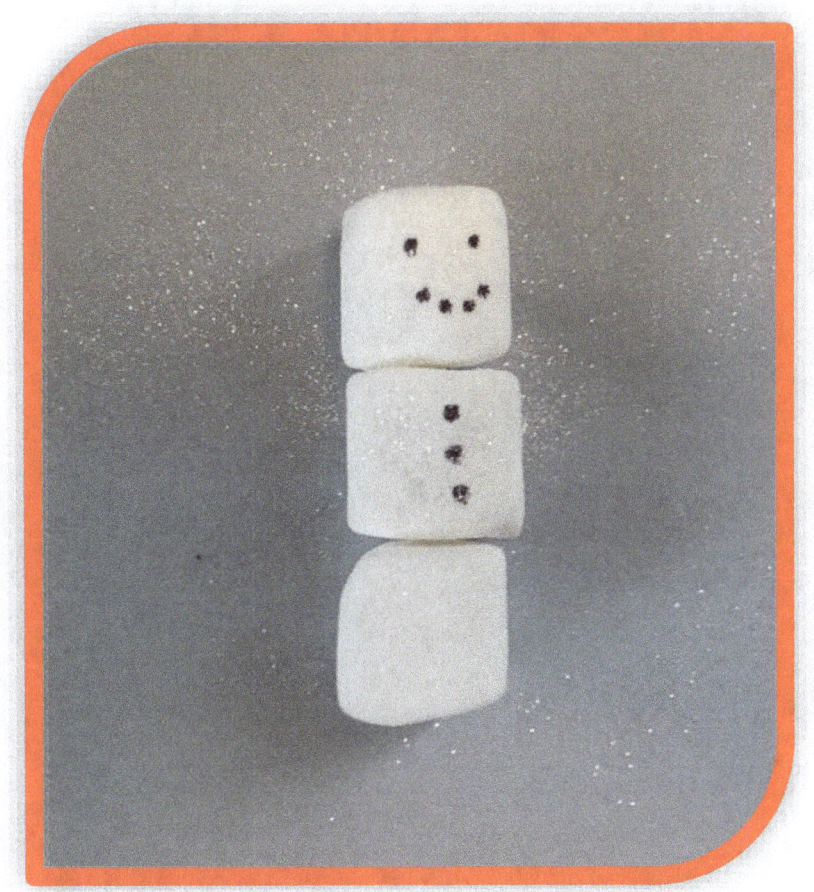

Instructions:

1. Lay out the surface protector.
2. Lay out the blue construction paper.
3. Help your child glue 3 marshmallows, one atop another to the construction paper, making a snowman.
4. Have your child put some dots of glue all over the paper.
5. Help your child sprinkle the paper with silver glitter to create a snowman in the snow. (*optional)

Making real-world connections with an
Accompanying activity, to reinforce learning and show children how art relates to their daily lives.
- *Read:* **Daniel plays in the snow.**

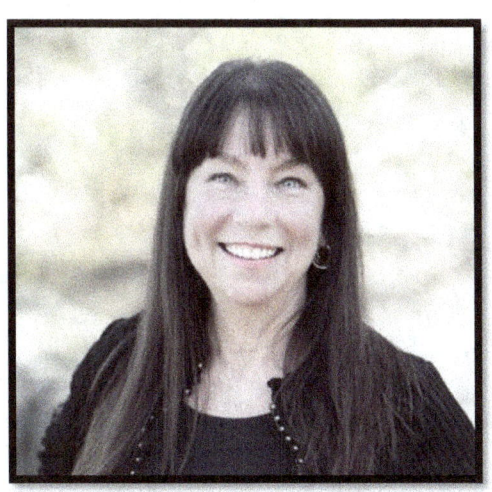
Photo by Kate Messer Photography

Katherine has been side by side with young children since she was ten years old. Starting out as a helper in her father's childcare center gave her hands-on experience with infants through school-agers!

She attended Western Kentucky University and graduated Magna Cum Laude with a bachelor's degree in art education.

Katherine has over thirty-five years of experience with children which includes teaching art in public and vocational schools, teaching in the Autism Unit, and working with preschoolers in a variety of settings. She has worked as a professional artist and taught private art lessons. Preschool is her favorite age to teach! See full bio at: Thepreschoolartexpert.com

Because she saw the need for a quality art curriculum in the preschool area, Katherine created The Preschool Art Expert.

Read about the creation and philosophy of The Preschool Art Expert at: ThePreschoolArtExpert.com.

Introduction to Art for Toddlers and Preschoolers is written for the preschool teacher as a school curriculum and for parents as a home-based curriculum and activities book. It is also for homeschoolers. It is for every socio-economic group and Ethnicity. It is for mainstream children as well as those with special needs, as art speaks to everyone. It is a valuable tool for children to get an introduction to and a foundation in art to prepare for the world ahead.

It is written in a simple way so that parents, and teachers alike, with or without an art background, can easily teach art skills to their children and students.

Katherine has used many of these projects with children in and outside the classroom. Some are her own ideas, some are borrowed from other teachers, and some were found on Pinterest.

We hope you enjoy this book and spend many hours learning with your children!

compliance